# Scholastic World Cultures
# CANADA

*by Harold Troper*

**■▲ SCHOLASTIC INC.**

*Titles in This Series*
CANADA
CHINA
GREAT BRITAIN
THE INDIAN SUBCONTINENT
JAPAN
LATIN AMERICA
MEXICO
THE MIDDLE EAST
SOUTHEAST ASIA
THE SOVIET UNION AND EASTERN EUROPE
TROPICAL AND SOUTHERN AFRICA

---

ISBN 0-590-34411-0

Copyright © 1985 by Scholastic Inc.
All rights reserved.
Published by Scholastic Book Services,
a division of Scholastic Inc.
Printed in the U.S.A.
12  11  10  9  8  7  6  5  4  3  2          0/9  1  2  3  4  5/9
                                                          23

Dr. Harold Troper is professer of history at the Ontario Institute for Studies in Education. He enjoys visiting the United States, and he loves the multi-ethnic hustle and bustle of Toronto. He is co-author of the bestseller *None Is Too Many.*

*Editorial Director, Text Division: Eleanor Angeles*
*Project Editor: Carolyn Jackson*
*Production Editor: Sarah Swartz*
*Double-Check: Sarah Swartz*
*Skills: Elma Schemenauer, Barbara Sack*
*Art Director: Kathryn Cole*
*Design and Maps: Yüksel Hassan*
*Photo Researcher: Nick Stephens*

---

COVER: Enthusiastic Canadians wave an outsized flag in the capital city of Ottawa during the ceremonies marking the patriation of the Canadian Constitution.

# CANADA

Books are never the creation of an author alone. This is no less true of this text. I am especially indebted to Adrian Peetoom for his trust, Sarah Swartz and Barbara Sack for their insight, Margaret Brennan for her tireless and good-natured labor on my behalf, and the Department of History and Philosophy at OISE for providing so positive a work environment.

H.T.

# Table of Contents

*Americans should never underestimate the constant pressure on Canada which the mere presence of the United States has produced. We're a different people from you, and we're a different people partly because of you. . . . Living next to you is in some ways like sleeping with an elephant. No matter how friendly and even-tempered is the beast, if I can call it that, one is affected by every twitch and grunt . . . . it should not therefore be expected that this kind of a nation, this Canada, should project itself . . . as a mirror image of the United States.*

FORMER PRIME MINISTER PIERRE TRUDEAU
IN AN ADDRESS TO THE NATIONAL PRESS
CLUB, WASHINGTON, D.C., 1969

# CANADA IN NORTH AMERICA

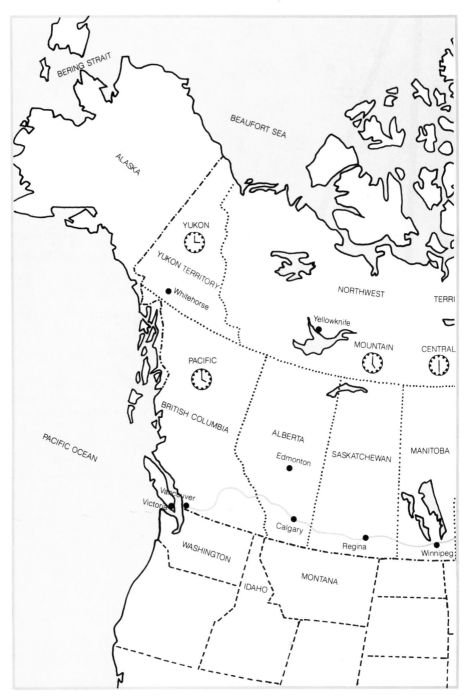

THE TRANS-CANADA HIGHWAY

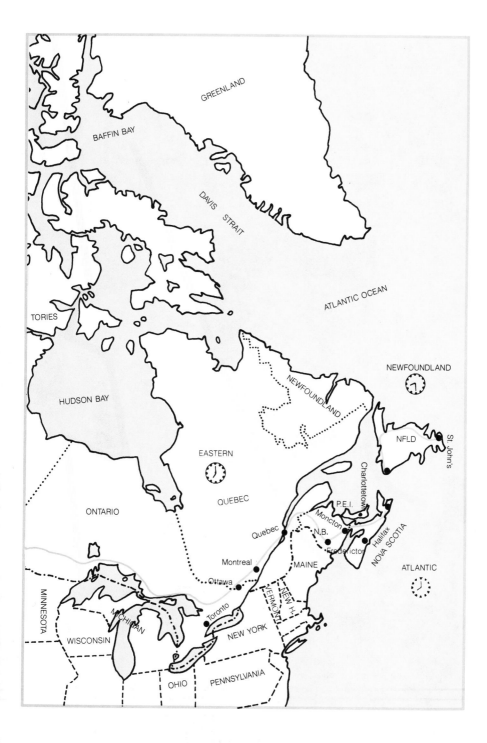

# 1
# THE NATION

CHILDREN · OF · A · COMMON · MOTHER

# Chapter 1

# Neighbor to the North

The Canadian correspondent for an American news-paper was recently asked what he felt was his most difficult problem in reporting from Canada. He is, he explained with modesty, a seasoned foreign correspon-dent. His job is to sort out and report events from places that are often distant from and alien to his readers. In covering some of the world's hot spots, he has seen the violence of war and the pain of human suffering. He has described revolutions, hunger, and innocent refugees fleeing in search of safety. His readers have learned about explosive events in lands where the language, religious tradition, standard of living, and culture are very different from their own.

Now he is stationed in Canada, and covering Canada is a different experience indeed. He is no longer writing about death squads, revolutions in the making, or bread shortages. Much of what he has found there seems hardly foreign to American eyes. Canada is a democracy. It is concerned with the rights of the individual, and guarantees equality for minorities. The general standard of living is much like that in the United States. The Canadian way of life — the way most Canadians dress, the cars they drive, how they earn their living, what they read or watch on TV, what they buy at their local supermarkets — differs little from that of most Americans in the same economic situation.

These similarities can be deceptive, however. Though the two countries have much in common, they remain separate and distinct. No matter how similar communities in the United States and Canada seem to the casual observer, one soon finds a deep Canadian pride in the uniqueness of its society. Canadians harbor a strong determination to chart their own course in North America.

But with so much in common, so many shared values, what is the best way to communicate the special character of Canadian society? This, the correspondent explained, is his most difficult problem.

Because Canada is so close, so familiar, so friendly and so peaceful, it is easy to take the country and its people for granted. This, the correspondent is convinced, is a dangerous error. Events in Canada, and the economic and political decisions Canadians make every day touch the lives of Americans as well. The United States cannot afford to ignore Canada. Canada is so important and close a neighbor that ignorance is intolerable. Too much is at stake.

The United States and Canada are locked together by a shared border running almost 4,000 miles (6,400 kilometers). It has often been called the "longest undefended border in the world." For this reason, it is important to understand each other's land, history, people, and problems. While both countries have equal stakes in the destiny of this continent, Canadians have their own priorities. Continued friendship between the two countries depends on mutual respect. Knowledge is a key part of that process.

Canada is a proud self-governing country. It is the United States' single largest trading partner and its closest ally. It is a member of NATO and other international alliances with the United States. However, it has made and will continue to make its own decisions in international affairs. During the Vietnam War, American draft resisters were allowed into Canada. It remains a close ally, but a firmly independent one. It demands to be treated as an equal.

In studying Canada, we can also learn something about the United States. Both countries are new nations. Both have matured into modern industrial countries from a colonial past. Both are today free and democratic societies. But Canada has chosen to follow its own path to national development. It is shaping its democratic institutions, forming a unique national identity, and wrestling with the problems of growth in a different way. With more knowledge of the Canadian experience, the American experience may come into clearer focus.

*This modern steel plant in Hamilton, Ontario, employs thousands of people.*

As Canadians know well, the United States is today the most powerful country in the world. Its economic, political, and cultural influence reaches every corner of the globe. Perhaps nowhere in the world, however, does that influence fall so heavily as it does on Canada. Canadians have long struggled to maintain their own identity and develop their own culture in the face of the neighboring American colossus. This has not always been easy.

By studying Canada we may begin to see the impact, for good and bad, that the United States can have on even the friendliest of allies. As Canadians know best of all, being an enemy of the United States can be dangerous. Being a friend has its own difficulties.

# Chapter 2

# Land of Diversity

Canada is the second largest country in the world. It covers an area of 3,851,809 square miles (9,975,594 square kilometers). It is larger than the United States, China, or Australia. A flight from St. John's, Newfoundland, on the Atlantic coast, to Victoria, British Columbia, on the Pacific, would be longer than one from St. John's to Rome in Italy. It would be longer than one southward to Bolivia, or northward beyond the North Pole. Western Europe could be set down in Canada five times, with room to spare.

From east to west, the country has six different time zones. The continental United States has only four. When Canadians in the most easterly part of the country are sitting down for lunch, most people on the west coast have not even climbed out of bed yet.

You might be surprised not only by Canada's size, but also by its diversity. As in the United States, differences in climate, geography, vegetation, traditions, and lifestyles abound. Any idea that the whole of

Canada is the same, or that all Canadians are alike, is wrong. Picture someone from outer space landing for a day in New York City and concluding that every corner of the United States is exactly like that city. What an argument there would be between this visitor and another from the same expedition if the second landed in the Grand Canyon.

**Geography.** Like the United States, Canada spans the continent from the Atlantic to the Pacific. But Canada has a third ocean coast — the Arctic. Its land crosses the Arctic Circle in the north. Its most southerly tip, Pelee Island, sits on the same latitude as northern California, almost halfway between the equator and the North Pole.

## MAJOR PHYSICAL CHARACTERISTICS

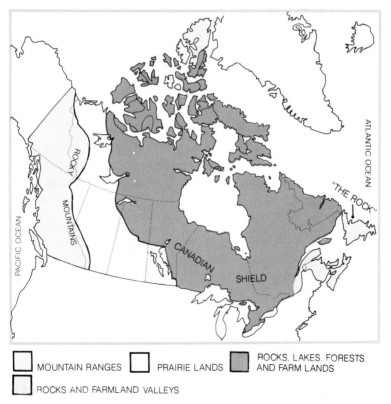

☐ MOUNTAIN RANGES  ☐ PRAIRIE LANDS  ▨ ROCKS, LAKES, FORESTS AND FARM LANDS

☐ ROCKS AND FARMLAND VALLEYS

Flying south from the far polar reaches of the Canadian North, you would first look down on a barren, frozen wilderness called *tundra*. The tundra would gradually give way to vast pine forests. Everywhere, you would see bare-faced rock and countless small lakes carved out of the earth during the last Ice Age.

But Canada is far more than wilderness. Farther south, forests are gradually replaced by farmlands or prairies. The rolling farmlands of southeastern Canada and the flat prairies of western Canada lie in sharp contrast to the majestic Rocky Mountains at the western edge of the prairies. The snow-capped Rockies, broken by large fertile valleys, are bordered on the west by a narrow coastal plain and the Pacific Ocean.

**Climate.** Canada's climate is characterized by extreme variations. While the polar regions are used to permanent winter, the southern Pacific coast is relatively mild. There, an umbrella gets far more use than a snow shovel. On the prairies, as on the neighboring plains of the United States, winter can be very severe. Wise drivers plug their cars' block heaters into electric outlets to ensure that their motors will not freeze and refuse to start. In some areas, the snowmobile is a more reliable form of winter transportation than the car.

The prairie deep-freeze doesn't always last. A sudden warming wind off the Rockies can change temperatures dramatically. Chinook winds (*chinook* comes from the Salish Indian word for "snow eater") can raise temperatures on the western prairies as much as 50°F (10°C) in a few minutes. Melting snow sometimes causes sudden floods. Chinooks also offer local residents a welcome, if usually temporary, break in the cold. Folk stories tell of prairie pioneers racing home in a horse-drawn sled ahead of a chinook wind. While the front of the sled rode on deep snow, the rear dragged in the mud.

People who live in the lower Great Lakes region, along the south shore of the St. Lawrence River, or on the Atlantic coast experience winters much like those in the nearby United States. Sometimes their winters are even less harsh. Toronto is only a short distance north of Buffalo and Rochester, New York, or Cleveland, Ohio. It experiences similar temperatures, but usually receives only a fraction of their snowfall. In the past, Toronto has lent its snow-removal equipment to Buffalo to help that snowbelt city dig out from under.

No U.S. winter weather forecast seems complete without warnings of another cold front moving in from Canada. But you may be surprised to learn that in summer most Canadians suffer long, humid heatwaves pushing in from the American South. They joke about U.S. tourists driving across the border in July, snow skis strapped to their cars. These tourists would be better off if they brought water skis instead, to use on the countless lakes and rivers in the vacation areas to which many Canadians escape during the summer heat.

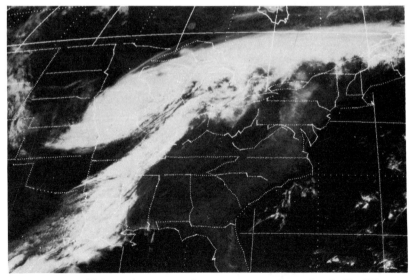

*Yet another warm front moves up from the Gulf of Mexico into eastern Canada.*

**Population and lifestyle.** Extremes in geography and climate have led to a very uneven spread of people across Canada's vast territory. The country has a population only about one-tenth that of the United States. As a result of its immense size, there is a very low population density — about four persons per square mile (1.61 square kilometer).

But this figure is misleading. Few Canadians live alone, isolated from their nearest neighbor. The population is actually very concentrated. More than three-quarters of all Canadians live within a narrow 200-mile (320-kilometer) strip of territory that hugs the American border.

Canadians tend to be a very urban people. More than 75 percent live in towns or cities. One-quarter of the total population lives in either Metropolitan Montreal or Metropolitan Toronto. Because of the relatively small number of people, these cities are proportionately very large. Like Americans, hundreds of thousands of Canadians take subways or buses to and from work or school. Few have ever seen a dogsled outside a museum.

Not all Canadians live in cities, however. Often, big yellow schoolbuses bring children from the surrounding countryside into small farm communities for school. The family may drive to town to shop, to have pieces of farm equipment repaired, or simply to enjoy a movie or a visit with friends.

Fishing villages along the Atlantic and Pacific coasts nurture an old way of life tied to the sea. But change is evident. Modern equipment, fish storage facilities, and increased competition from overseas fishermen are changing the life in these communities.

In the Canadian interior, there are many mining and one-industry towns. Here the fortunes of the community rise and fall with those of the major employer. It might be a mining company, a lumbering company, or a manufacturing concern. If markets and sales are good, everyone prospers. If not, the whole town suffers. In a copper-mining town, a drastic fall in the export price of copper can quickly threaten a thriving community with becoming a ghost town.

**Language.** French and English are the official languages of the country, although not all Canadians speak both. French is the main language spoken in Quebec and other regions with a heavy French-Canadian population. English is the prime language of the rest of Canada.

Native languages are still spoken with pride by many native people. Recent immigrants and their children often use their own language to communicate with

*Enjoying a walk along a typical street in Montreal, largest city in the province of Quebec.*

family and friends. In Toronto, which has received tens of thousands of immigrants in the past 35 years, it is estimated that more than 70 languages or dialects are commonly spoken. Riding in a Toronto subway car, you are likely to hear people speaking in Chinese, Yiddish, Greek, Spanish, Italian, Portuguese, and Hindi. Foreign-language newspapers abound.

**Canadian identity.** Today there are almost 25 million people who call Canada home. These people are the country's most important resource. Canada is their land. Its history is their history.

But who are these Canadians? If you were asked to draw a picture of a Canadian, could you do it? What image comes to your mind when you hear the word "Canadian"?

Is it a red-coated police officer standing smartly at attention? If that is the case, you will be disappointed. Only a few RCMP officers are assigned to wear their dress uniforms, and only for official occasions. The RCMP today serves as the federal police force in Canada, much like the FBI in the United States. They also act as provincial police in most provinces. Anyone who deals with an RCMP officer is likely to face a man or woman in a business suit or, on the highway, in a smart brown uniform.

Do you picture a lumberjack with a plaid jacket swinging a huge ax? The lumbering industry remains very important to Canada, but the legendary lumberjack, ax in hand, is history. Power saws have replaced the ax, and huge machines that cut the trees, then strip and stack the timber, are today replacing the power saw. Rather than the lumberjacks of old, you are likely to find hard-working men and women with important technical skills. Increasingly, those in the lumber industry need college courses as much as powerful muscles and strong backs.

*A keen lookout on a dock in Seal Cove, Grand Manan Island, New Brunswick.*

NATIONAL UKRAINIAN FESTIVAL

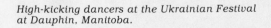

*High-kicking dancers at the Ukrainian Festival at Dauphin, Manitoba.*

In fact, Canadians are known for their great diversity in culture and heritage. Many are of British or French descent. They or their ancestors came from the British Isles or France. Millions of Canadians, however, are of neither British nor French origin. Canada contains people of almost every background and culture. Immigration, especially mass immigration during the last 30 years, has shaped and reshaped the population. Less than four percent of the people are of native origin.

Canadian society is seen as a "mosaic," a diverse collection of cultural traditions existing side by side, in harmony. In an atmosphere of mutual respect for their varied backgrounds, Canadians are attempting to create national unity through cultural diversity. There may be only one Canada, but there are many ways to be Canadian.

**Regionalism.** Canadian geography has encouraged the emergence of distinct regions and regional loyalties. The Atlantic Provinces region, which is greatly influenced by the sea, consists of the provinces of Newfoundland and Labrador, Nova Scotia, New Brunswick, and Prince Edward Island. (A province is much the same as a state.) Some people consider Newfoundland and Labrador a region of its own and lump the other three together as the Maritime Provinces. French-speaking Quebec and industrial Ontario make up the region of Central Canada. The agricultural Prairie region includes Manitoba, Saskatchewan, and Alberta. The mountainous province of British Columbia is referred to as the Pacific West Coast region. The vast region of the Canadian North includes the Yukon and the Northwest Territories.

Each region has its own flavor and its own way of life. Each has its different interests based on diverse geography, climate, language, and people. Together they make up Canada.

# Double-check

## Review

**1.** How many time zones does Canada have?

**2.** Name the three oceans that border Canada.

**3.** What is the size of Canada's population, and how does it compare with that of the United States?

**4.** What fraction of the Canadian population lives within 200 miles (320 kilometers) of the U.S. border?

**5.** What percentage of all Canadians live in towns or cities?

## Discussion

**1.** Discuss several reasons for studying about Canada. Why are the United States and Canada such friendly neighbors? What problems do you think might arise between them?

**2.** What are the problems of living in a large country? How is it different from living in a small country? What do Canada and the United States have in common because they are so large? How are they different in spite of this similarity?

**3.** What does "bilingual" mean? Name some other countries that are officially bilingual or multilingual. How many students in your class speak more than one language?

## Activities

**1.** Some students might pretend to be a reporter for an international newspaper, sent to Canada on assignment. They could write a short article for the paper to introduce their readers to Canada.

**2.** Some might pretend they have moved from a rural area on the Canadian prairies to a large eastern Canadian city such as Montreal. They could write a letter to a friend describing their new life: what kind of home they have, how they get to school, what they do for fun, who their friends and neighbors are, what the weather is like. Or they might imagine they have moved to a farm in Saskatchewan, and write to a friend in the city.

**3.** Three or four students might prepare a skit in which they pretend to be people from another planet who have visited different parts of Canada — perhaps the Arctic, an Atlantic fishing community, and Toronto. The visitors could discuss their experiences, ending the skit with some resolution about what Canada is *really* like.

# Skills

## SOME POPULATION FIGURES

| Population by provinces and territories (1981) (in thousands) | |
| --- | --- |
| Newfoundland | 568 |
| Prince Edward Island | 123 |
| Nova Scotia | 847 |
| New Brunswick | 696 |
| Quebec | 6,438 |
| Ontario | 8,625 |
| Manitoba | 1,026 |
| Saskatchewan | 968 |
| Alberta | 2,238 |
| British Columbia | 2,744 |
| Yukon | 23 |
| Northwest Territories | 46 |
| Canada | 24,343 |

| Population by age groups (1980) (in thousands) | |
| --- | --- |
| Under 15 | 5,500 |
| 0-4 | 1,784 |
| 5-9 | 1,776 |
| 10-14 | 1,941 |
| 15-64 | 16,154 |
| 15-19 | 2,360 |
| 20-24 | 2,332 |
| 25-34 | 4,055 |
| 35-44 | 2,837 |
| 45-54 | 2,471 |
| 55-64 | 2,099 |
| 65+ | 2,282 |

Source: Statistics Canada

*Use the charts above and information in Chapter 2 to answer the following questions.*

1. What do the above charts represent?

2. What was the population of Newfoundland in 1981? Of the Yukon?

3. Which province had the highest population? Which had the second highest? Why are these two provinces most heavily populated?

4. Into which age group did you fit in 1980: 0-4, 5-9, or 10-14? How many Canadians were in that age group then?

5. What was the largest age group of Canadians in 1980? What was the smallest?

# 2
# ACROSS CANADA

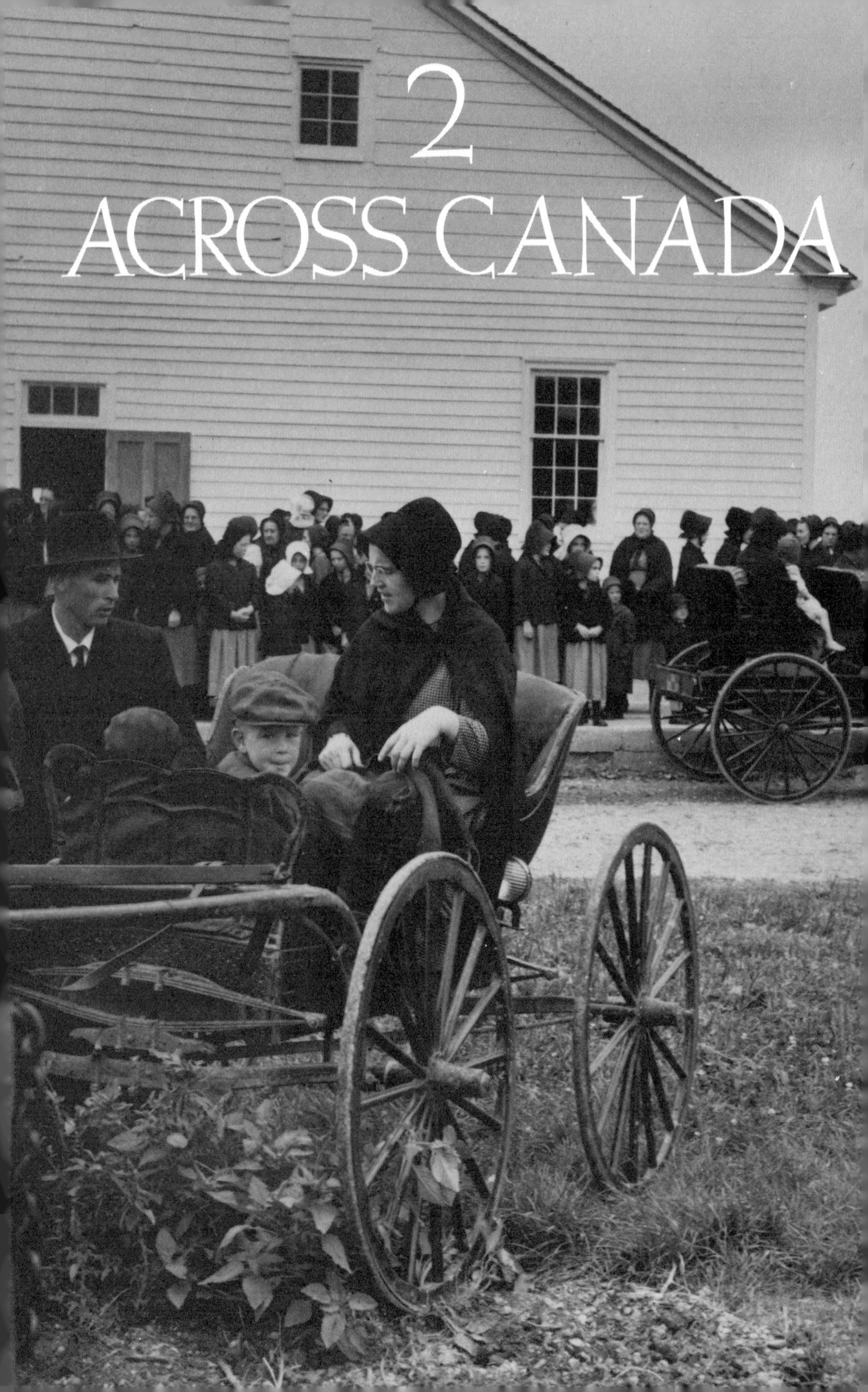

# Chapter 3

# Atlantic Canada

Since Canada is a sparsely populated, vast land of great contrasts, what binds it together? What is the best way to understand a country where variations and contrasts are the rule? One way is to travel through it. Let us imagine ourselves driving across Canada together.

This is not a trip to be taken lightly. Driving from the Atlantic coast on the east to the Pacific coast on the west is a very long journey. We will follow the most direct route, the Trans-Canada Highway, taking a side trip here and there. If we drive 10 hours a day at 55 miles (88 kilometers) an hour, it will still take us more than eight days to make the trip. In the end, we will have traveled well over 4,000 miles (6,400 kilometers) and have covered all 10 provinces that make up the country. The Trans-Canada Highway, like the two transcontinental railways, the Canadian Pacific and the Canadian National, links Canadians with one another. It weaves through the areas with the highest population density, carrying Canadians and the goods they produce right across the country.

25

Even allowing ourselves some short side trips, we will not see all of the country. Vast areas are still inaccessible by road, rail, or boat. These areas must be entered by aircraft, sometimes specially equipped to land on water or snow.

**Newfoundland and Labrador.** Our journey begins in Canada's most easterly city, St. John's, Newfoundland, the capital and largest city of the province. Newfoundland is a triangular-shaped island of roughly 42,000 square miles (110,000 square kilometers). It juts out into the Atlantic at the wide mouth of the Gulf of St. Lawrence.

The island is just far enough east of the mainland to require its own time zone. It is not far enough east, however, to require a full hour's difference. As a result, clocks in Newfoundland are set only half an hour later than those on the nearest mainland. A classic Canadian joke warns, "The world will end at midnight, 12:30 in Newfoundland."

As throughout the Atlantic region, fishing remains an economic mainstay. Most of the island's people live in St. John's or along the northeast shoreline, which is honeycombed with small, sheltered harbors and bays. For generations, Newfoundland's fiercely independent people have sailed to the nearby Grand Banks, where they fish for cod. The fish were once so numerous that folk tales tell of a time, long ago, when fishermen had trouble plying their small wooden boats through waters thick with fish. Today, the fisheries still employ numerous Newfoundlanders. But decreased world demand for fish, and competition from foreign factory boats have greatly reduced fish stocks. This has hurt the local fishing industry. Lumbering and mining now rival fishing as the most important industry.

St. John's is one of North America's oldest cities. It is also the nearest North American city to Europe. Economic life centers on the waterfront where boats are repaired, supplies are bought, and produce is exported. As we leave the city, with the harbor behind us, we see Signal Hill where in 1901 Marconi received the first transatlantic wireless radio message.

The highway makes an enormous arch to the north across the island. We pass many small fishing villages, called outports, nestled in coastal inlets. We pass barren landscape that offers no hope for farming. We understand why so many Newfoundlanders call their island "the Rock." The road skirts the almost completely uninhabited forests and bogs that make up most of the island's interior. As we move west, we drive past small mining and lumbering towns.

To the northwest, across the Strait of Belle Isle, lies Labrador. Although it is on the mainland, it is part of what is officially called the province of Newfoundland and Labrador. Its small population and rough terrain

*The first transatlantic radio message was received here from Cornwall, England. The inset shows Marconi.*

*Overlooking one of the fine sheltered harbors
on Canada's east coast, St. John's, Newfoundland.*

make travel by car difficult. For many years, before the
advent of transatlantic jet travel, Labrador was the first
and last stop for propeller aircraft crossing the ocean.
Nearly all planes landed at Goose Bay in Labrador to
refuel.

As we drive south along the west coast of the island,
we finally reach Port-aux-Basques, on the southwest
tip. Here we board the ferry for a seven-hour trip to the
mainland.

**Nova Scotia.** After a choppy voyage, the ferry pulls
into North Sidney at the north tip of Cape Breton
Island in Nova Scotia. We find ourselves in a mining
town where coal and steel production dominate the
economy. In many mining areas it is possible to tour
local coal mines, but not here. Safety regulations pro-
hibit tourists from entering these mines, and with
good reason. The mines in the Sydney area begin on
land, but the shafts soon follow the coal fields out
under the Atlantic. Some of the shafts reach as much
as four miles (6.5 kilometers) out under the ocean floor.

Less than an hour's drive east from Sydney is the old Fortress of Louisbourg. Just over 200 years ago, the French built Louisbourg to defend their colonies in North America. The large French fishing fleet found safety and took on supplies in the Louisbourg harbor. French pirates, who preyed on colonial New England merchant vessels to the south, also made harbor in the shadow of the fortress. In 1758, Louisbourg was captured by the British. They demolished the fortress to prevent it from again threatening British colonial life.

Today Louisbourg is an important historical site. Much of the fortress and the surrounding town have been reconstructed from the original plans. Guides in period costumes take us through the buildings. We sample food cooked the way it was two centuries ago. We get a feeling of what life must have been like in this distant French colony.

Back in our car, we return to the Trans-Canada Highway. As we move southward across Cape Breton Island, we cannot help but notice that the ocean shapes life for the people of Nova Scotia. This is also true of its sister provinces, New Brunswick and Prince Edward Island.

The Maritime Provinces, as they are often called, have not kept economic pace with the rest of Canada. Together with Newfoundland, the Maritimes have been plagued with unemployment and slow economic development. Fishing, mining, farming, and lumbering are important to the local economies. However, there is still not enough work for those who want it.

Our drive across Cape Breton takes us past forested, flat-topped hills that seem to rise suddenly out of the sea. Gradually the forest thins out. Before long, we are crossing farmlands. The highway leads us to the Canso Causeway and across to the mainland of Nova Scotia.

*A mighty container ship leaving Halifax harbor.*

*Peggy's Cove, a favorite spot for artists and photographers.*

*Ready for a big catch.*

*Nova Scotia — water, water everywhere!*

A side trip to Nova Scotia's capital, Halifax, reveals a busy port city with one of the best deep-water harbors in the world. The modern city is built out from the harbor. It now surrounds steep Citadel Hill, once defended by British cannons. Today, the harbor shelters a modern naval base and a container port that ships Canadian goods to the world.

Halifax has lots of shopping and entertainment facilities, but we must soon leave. We continue our side trip south along the coast and visit the scenic rocky crags of Peggy's Cove. In this quiet village, boats drawn up on shore and wooden lobster traps piled high remind us how important fishing is to the local economy. We also realize how dangerous boating in these waters can be when we see the old lighthouse. It stands on a massive, windswept granite ledge jutting out into the Atlantic.

A little farther south, we reach the town of Lunenburg, one of the great fishing ports on the continent. Lunenburg was once a major shipbuilding center. Its most famous boat was the *Bluenose*. This sleek wooden vessel was the pride of the Nova Scotia fishing fleet and four-time winner of international schooner races. The original *Bluenose* no longer exists, but it was so important that the schooner's likeness is now engraved on the back of the Canadian dime. Even today Nova Scotians are sometimes referred to as "bluenosers."

We drive eastward, back to the Trans-Canada. We skirt the more densely populated southern farming area. We pass the large, fertile Annapolis valley, where fruit orchards stand in sharp contrast to the surrounding forested slopes.

**Prince Edward Island.** An alternate route, this time by ferry, takes us across the Northumberland Strait to long, narrow Prince Edward Island in the southern Gulf of St. Lawrence. P.E.I., as it is called, is the smallest but most densely populated Canadian province. Intensive farming, especially of potatoes, dominates the island's rolling landscape, with its rich red soil. In addition, P.E.I. has a profitable lobster-fishing industry. Tourists flock to the island's beautiful red-tinted sand beaches.

**New Brunswick.** Back on the mainland, we drive into New Brunswick, the largest Maritime province. At Chignecto Bay on the Bay of Fundy, we stop to watch the tide sweep in from the Atlantic. At low tide, streams draining into the bay are almost dry. As the highest tide in the world rushes in, it raises the water levels as much as 52 feet (16 meters). The stream beds fill with tidal water till they seem to flow backward. Every day, the Fundy tide pushes a weight of water into the bay 70 times greater than the weight of water discharged by the Mississippi River into the Gulf of Mexico.

Not far beyond Chignecto Bay, we drive through the city of Moncton, a railway center. What interests us most as we go north beyond the city is Magnetic Hill, just off the highway. Here, we park our car at what looks like the bottom of a hill, next to a white post. We turn off our motor and put the car into neutral. To our surprise, the car begins to coast "uphill," as if drawn by

*Thousands of American tourists visit this spot each year.*

*A major tourist attraction in Moncton, New Brunswick. Notice the bilingual sign.*

a mysterious force counteracting gravity. Of course this is not really the case. We are caught in the middle of a huge optical illusion. What seems to our eye to be the "bottom" of the hill is not. As we coast down, our eye incorrectly tells us we are moving uphill.

From Moncton, we drive to Fredericton, New Brunswick's capital. This small city is situated on the broad, flat, fertile plain of the St. John River. As we drive out of the hills onto the flat lands below, it seems as if the water on the low, marshy land could easily wash over the road. In the distance, terraced farmlands dominate the gentle valley slopes.

Beyond Fredericton, the highway snakes along the riverbank, passing through farmlands. As we turn north, the valley begins to narrow, with steep hills rising on either side of the river. Sometimes we see boats pulling log-booms, huge rafts of timber cut in the forested interior. The timber is brought to the river to float downstream to lumber mills.

As we move northward, we notice another change. The English-language signs, billboards, and place names are mixed with others in French.

# Double-check

## Review

1. How long does it take to drive across Canada on the Trans-Canada Highway?

2. How many provinces make up Canada?

3. Name Canada's most easterly city. In which province is it located?

4. Why is farming a major industry in Prince Edward Island? For what produce is P.E.I. best known?

5. What are the main industries in New Brunswick?

## Discussion

1. What different types of transportation could a person use to travel across Canada? What are the advantages and disadvantages of each? When would it be best to use each? Why is transportation so important in binding a nation together?

2. Look at a map to see what Newfoundland, Prince Edward Island, and Cape Breton have in common geographically. How does this geographic similarity affect the lives of the people who live there?

3. Discuss the economic problems of the Maritime provinces. Why do you think the unemployment rate in this region is so high? Why do many Maritimers live in other parts of Canada?

## Activities

1. Students might create a wall display with pictures of places along the Trans-Canada Highway from St. John's, Newfoundland, to Victoria, British Columbia. (A travel agency, a Canadian tourism office or a Canadian Embassy or Consulate might be helpful sources.) A good title should be found for the display.

2. Some students might want to read the classic *Anne of Green Gables*, which tells the story of a young orphan girl who goes to live in Prince Edward Island. They could report to the class on what life was like in a small Maritime community at the turn of the century.

3. Some students might write a diary entry, describing one day's journey through the Atlantic provinces.

## *Skills*

## THE TRANS-CANADA HIGHWAY

*Use the map on pages 6-7 and information in Chapter 3 to answer the following questions.*

1. What does the colored line on the map represent? What do the unbroken lines represent?

2. The Trans-Canada Highway runs closest to which border of Canada?
   (a) northern  (b) eastern  (c) southern

3. About how long is the Trans-Canada Highway?
   (a) 4,000 miles (6,400 kilometers)
   (b) 3,500 miles (5,600 kilometers)
   (c) 9,000 miles (14,500 kilometers)

4. Which two cities are the farthest north along the Trans-Canada?
   (a) Saskatoon and Edmonton
   (b) Saskatoon and St. John's
   (c) Edmonton and St. John's

5. Which city along the Trans-Canada is closest to Europe?
   (a) Vancouver  (b) St. John's  (c) Halifax

# Chapter 4

# Central Canada

Soon we leave the uplands of New Brunswick behind and cross into Canada's huge central region.

**Quebec.** Once we enter Quebec, the largest Canadian province, the highway descends to the gently rolling farmlands of the St. Lawrence River valley. At Rivière du Loup, where the highway meets the river, the St. Lawrence is 15 miles (24 kilometers) wide. It narrows very gradually as we follow it westward to Quebec City.

Driving along the Trans-Canada, we will merely skim Quebec's south edge. The province is twice the size of Texas. Much of it remains a vast frontier. Until recently, its forests, rocky lakes, and rivers were largely undeveloped. Today, mining, lumbering, and massive hydroelectric power plants challenge the quiet interior. This enormous area is part of the majestic horseshoe-shaped region known as the Canadian Shield.

As we drive up the valley, we pass many small towns, each with its church steeple outlined against the sky, and its long narrow farms that run down to the river's edge. Our eyes and ears become conscious of the

French language surrounding us. The signs we see are printed in French. People speak French on the car radio. We are in the heartland of French Canada, where French is the prime language.

Quebec City, the provincial capital, sits atop a steep bluff overlooking the St. Lawrence. It has two faces. It is an old walled city, the only one north of Mexico. But beyond the walls, it is also a modern, bustling twentieth-century city.

Within the old city, we walk the narrow cobblestone streets and marvel at the well-preserved buildings, built while Quebec was a French colony. But this is no museum. Far from it. Old Quebec is living and exciting, the heart of the city's cultural life. The streets are dotted with fine restaurants, cafés, shops, and bookstores. It is a feast for the eyes of visitors like ourselves. But it is simply home to the many Quebecers we pass on the winding streets.

*St. Denis Street in old Quebec City.*

*One of the most celebrated pilgrim areas in North America, Ste. Anne de Beaupré.*

Just beyond the walls stands the Quebec assembly building, seat of the provincial government. It is only a short walk from there to the Plains of Abraham. Here, in 1759, 17 years before the American Revolution, French and British troops fought a decisive battle. Where children play today, British attackers finally overwhelmed the French garrison defending the city. With the French defeat at the Plains of Abraham, Britain assumed control over the French colonial empire in North America.

Like New York's Manhattan, Montreal is built on an island. Also like Manhattan, as land became scarce, the only direction for city expansion was up. Today, office towers in the downtown core soar skyward. But the unique charm of this European-like French-speaking city has not been overwhelmed. The stately older residential neighborhoods and a picturesque section of old Montreal remain to balance the highrise core.

Until recently, the Roman Catholic Church was among the most important and powerful influences in the province of Quebec. That influence can be clearly seen in a visit to the Shrine of Ste. Anne de Beaupré, only a short drive east of the city. Shortly after the first chapel was built here in 1658, miraculous cures were reported among the sick who visited. Today, a shrine near where the original chapel stood attracts over a million pilgrims annually. They give thanks for their health or pray for recovery from illness. Catholic and non-Catholic visitors alike wonder at numerous crutches and braces that cover the walls. Each has reportedly been left at the shrine by someone who claimed to have found healing aid through prayer.

As we journey three hours southwest from Quebec City, the St. Lawrence River continues to narrow. On the south side, hills slope down to the valley below. To the north, the Laurentian Mountains of the Canadian Shield loom into view. Before long, the valley broadens out as it meets the south-flowing Ottawa River. On an island where the two rivers meet is the city of Montreal.

Greater Montreal is home to almost two and a half million people. It is largely French speaking, second only to Paris, France, as the largest French-speaking city in the world. Only in Montreal are announcements at major-league baseball games between the Montreal Expos and its National League rivals made first in French, then in English.

Winters can be very harsh in Montreal. One response to the ice and cold has been the recent development of what Montrealers call the underground city. A maze of modern, heated walkways cuts under the city streets. The walkways, lined with shops and restaurants, connect to both the Montreal subway system and buildings on the surface. It is possible to walk through much of Montreal's busy business core in winter without ever putting on a coat.

Montreal is also a port city. Ocean-going vessels sail up the St. Lawrence to Montreal, where they unload goods from all over the world for Canadian buyers. Then they take on Canadian cargoes for export to the rest of the world.

In summer, however, ships can now sail far inland beyond Montreal, through the St. Lawrence Seaway. The Seaway is a system of locks and canals serving both the United States and Canada. It permits ocean-going vessels to sail from the Atlantic Ocean through the Great Lakes and into the heart of the continent — a 1,300 mile (2,100 kilometer) voyage. It gives the industrial North American interior a direct shipping link with the rest of the world.

**Ontario.** From Montreal we go north along the Ottawa River, which marks the border between French-speaking and English-speaking Canada. In a few hours we reach Ottawa, the nation's capital.

Like Washington, D.C., Ottawa is a government city. Canada's imposing parliament buildings face across the river to Quebec. They house the Canadian government. Ottawa and the adjoining city of Hull, in the province of Quebec, are filled with official buildings and national institutions. To the visitor, Ottawa seems less formal and more relaxed than Washington. Only a short drive from the city's center are the Gatineau Hills, where winter skiing attracts many enthusiasts, including politicians and government workers.

From Ottawa, we leave the Trans-Canada and drive south to the scenic Thousand Islands, where we stop for an afternoon cruise. Here Lake Ontario spills into the St. Lawrence River. Then we turn west and find ourselves on a broad, fertile agricultural plain running up from the lake's edge. We pass prosperous farms with their rich harvests of fruit and vegetables.

*The old parliament buildings
as they appeared in 1892.*

While this is some of the best farmland in Canada, it is also the most heavily urbanized and industrialized area in the country. One-third of all Canadians live in the narrow 550 mile (885 kilometer) strip of land between Montreal and Windsor, Ontario. As the population of this region grew, industry expanded. Farmland gave way to highways, housing, factories, and shopping centers. Today, efforts are underway to clean up pollution, and industrial growth is being regulated.

The urban explosion becomes most evident as we near Toronto. The highway grows in places from four to 16 lanes as we enter Canada's largest urban center. In recent years, Toronto and the surrounding area have mushroomed in size and population. Today, Metropolitan Toronto has over two and a half million people. This is due, in large part, to immigration from abroad.

*The world-famous CN Tower.*

*The Niagara Falls are more spectacular on the Canadian side of the river.*

*The elevators in Thunder Bay are even bigger than those in Duluth, Minnesota.*

The city's downtown is a startling contrast of older neighborhoods and modern skyscrapers. We take the elevator to the top of the CN Tower, the highest free-standing structure in the world. From there, we look out over the city and surprisingly far beyond, in every direction. To the south, we can see the United States a little more than 30 miles (48 kilometers) away.

Toronto is Canada's business and financial center. Head offices of business firms fill the modern downtown skyscrapers. Bay Street in Toronto, like Wall Street in New York, is seen as the country's economic center. Bloor Street, like New York's Fifth Avenue, is regarded as the center for fashion and style.

The hundreds of thousands of immigrants who have moved into Toronto have had an obvious impact. Different neighborhoods reflect waves of immigrants from all over the world. A huge Italian area, filled with shops selling Italian food specialties or simply advertising to customers in Italian, is matched on a smaller scale by Greek, Portuguese, Chinese, Hungarian, Polish, Caribbean, and Maltese neighborhoods, to name only a few. One of the special treats Toronto offers is to wander through these different areas. Our ears attune to the many languages being spoken as we stroll along and sample the food.

*Toronto's busy Kensington Market.*

We head north again, leaving behind the rich agricultural lands and the urban industrial complex of the lower Great Lakes. We drive into the Canadian Shield where rocky, forest-covered hills and countless small lakes fill our view. There are few people and even fewer farms.

The Canadian Shield sweeps southeasterly out of the Arctic. It reaches almost to the lower Great Lakes before it arches back toward the northeast, Quebec and the Atlantic. For much of Canadian history, the Shield formed a natural barrier to travel and to settlement of the western Canadian interior. This untamed land of rock, forest, marshy swamps, and lakes was also a magnet for lumbering and mining industries. As we drive into the mining town of Sudbury, the huge smokestack of the nickel smelter stands high against the sky. We drive past a mammoth nickel coin at the highway's edge. It is the symbol of the mining industry that dominates the local economy.

We continue to the northwest and marvel at the engineering effort it must have taken to construct this highway and the railway lines we parallel. Much of it had to be blasted through solid rock. The rough land is strikingly beautiful, especially as we pass Georgian Bay and go around the northern rim of Lake Superior. Steep hills, colorful granite rock formations, thick forests, and cascading rivers are in constant view. Every now and again, a road sign warns us that moose may suddenly dart across the highway. This is cottage and ski-chalet country.

At the western tip of Lake Superior, we drive into the city of Thunder Bay. This city, the most inland port of the St. Lawrence Seaway system, is a major exporter of grain. It contains some of the largest grain elevators in the world, and makes us aware of the prairies that lie ahead.

# Double-check

## Review

**1.** What is the prime language spoken in Quebec?

**2.** How does the province of Quebec compare in size with the state of Texas?

**3.** What historical event occurred in 1759 at the Plains of Abraham in Quebec City? Why was it so important?

**4.** Name Canada's capital city.

**5.** What is the highest free-standing structure in the world? Where is it located?

## Discussion

**1.** In what ways do you think life in Quebec might be different from life in the rest of Canada? How would it be the same? Explain your answers.

**2.** Why is the area stretching from Montreal, Quebec, in the east to Windsor, Ontario, in the west so heavily populated? Why are there fewer people farther west?

**3.** Discuss the problems caused by heavy urbanization and industrialization. Do you think industrial growth should be regulated? Why or why not?

## Activities

**1.** Some students might pretend to be touring Quebec City or Montreal. They could design a postcard to send to a friend at home, writing on the back a description of the sights they have visited.

**2.** The capital of Canada was moved every few years until 1865, when it became Ottawa. Students might research and report to the class about Ottawa's history, geography, and attractions, comparing it with Washington, D.C.

**3.** Groups of students might each choose an important city in Quebec or Ontario and list as many facts about it as possible: population, special attractions, types of industry, and so on. After all groups have presented their lists to the class, the lists might be combined to form a class chart.

# Skills

## SOME MAJOR CANADIAN CITIES

| | EDMONTON | HALIFAX | MONTREAL | TORONTO | VANCOUVER | WINNIPEG |
|---|---|---|---|---|---|---|
| 1. Population in thousands | 657 | 277 | 2828 | 2999 | 1268 | 585 |
| 2. Population as % of provincial population | 29% | 33% | 44% | 32% | 46% | 57% |
| 3. % of country's manufacturing | 2.6 | 0.7 | 13.6 | 18.1 | 4.4 | 1.9 |
| 4. Magazines published | 28 | 7 | 204 | 495 | 86 | 43 |
| 5. Newspaper circulation in thousands | 242 | 72 | 444 | 921 | 296 | 229 |
| 6. Number of theater companies | 6 | 1 | 31 | 32 | 14 | 4 |
| 7. Number of major sports teams | 3 | 0 | 4 | 4 | 3 | 2 |
| 8. Appeal to people from elsewhere | high | low | low | moderate | high | low |

Source: Statistics Canada

*Use the chart above and information in Chapter 4 to answer the following questions.*

1. Why are the above cities included in this chart?

2. In which general area of Canada are the two largest cities found?

3. Which city has the largest percentage of its province's population?

4. Which two cities are most attractive to people moving from other provinces? Why might that be?

5. Suppose you are a sports writer who writes for magazines and newspapers. In which city would you probably find the most work? How do you know?

# Chapter 5

# The Canadian West and the North

West of Thunder Bay, the highway presses on through the Canadian Shield. Finally, almost without warning, the land broadens out and we descend onto lowlands. We have reached the eastern edge of the Canadian prairies. From here, the prairies flow westward for approximately 800 miles (1,300 kilometers) to the Rocky Mountain foothills.

The provinces of Manitoba, Saskatchewan, and Alberta, together with British Columbia and the Canadian North, provide the last large area for Canadian expansion. For years, their growth seemed dependent on investment money from Ontario and Quebec. As a result, western Canadians resented eastern Canada's economic domination of western development.

Today, however, those roles have changed. The Canadian West is rich in resources. It not only has agricultural production, it also has abundant energy resources, mining, and lumbering. The new wealth in the Canadian West and prospects for massive development in the Canadian North have brought pride and self-confidence to those areas. The West is the new economic force to be reckoned with in Canada today.

**Manitoba.** Driving across the province of Manitoba at first seems strange to us. We have just driven out of the rough Canadian Shield. The Trans-Canada no longer snakes through a wilderness of forests, lakes, and rocky hills. It now runs flat and smooth, in a straight line. Driving westward into the bright setting sun makes us stop at a service center and buy a pair of good sunglasses.

On either side of the highway, the rich black farmland stretches as far as the eye can see. Few trees break the horizon. Farmhouses are far apart, indicating the large size of the western farms.

In the southeastern corner of this prairie expanse, where the Red and Assiniboine Rivers meet, is the city of Winnipeg, the capital of Manitoba. This large city, like the surrounding countryside, is flat. Those who fly into Winnipeg at night say that from above it looks like a bejeweled spider's web spreading out into the prairie blackness.

Winnipeg was once called "the gateway to the Canadian West." As we explore it, the reason soon becomes clear. It is an isolated city, a great distance from any city of similar size. It is also a major transportation center. The Trans-Canada Highway and all railway traffic to and from eastern Canada pass through Winnipeg. Almost all the hundreds of thousands of settlers who moved west stopped there. It was to the Canadian West what Chicago was to the American Midwest and the prairie states.

*Winnipeg is a friendly cosmopolitan city of 600,000, built around the Red and Assiniboine Rivers.*

That era is over. Highway and railway traffic still make Winnipeg a communications hub. But the advent of jet air traffic and the recent economic growth of other western cities have overshadowed it. Yet, Winnipeg is special. Because they were isolated from other cities, Winnipegers were forced to rely on themselves. With a population of just over half a million people, the city houses world-class ballet and opera companies, a symphony orchestra, live theater, and other cultural institutions that are the envy of cities many times its size.

As a side trip, we drive north to nearby Lake Winnipeg. Here the Canadian Shield and the prairie meet again. This lake and the surrounding countryside offer tourists a host of outdoor activities in both summer and winter.

Lake Winnipeg and the river system of which it is a part eventually drain into Hudson Bay far to the north. In summer, when there is no fear of being frozen in the

*Life up here is boring. Thank goodness for tourists!*

ice, ships enter the bay. They take on a cargo of grain at Canada's most northerly port, Churchill, at the mouth of the Churchill River. That city is on the migratory route for polar bears. In the autumn, migrating bears have been known to wander past the city limits in search of food. You can understand why local citizens become very cautious about walking around town, especially at night.

**Saskatchewan and Alberta.** We follow the highway due west out of Winnipeg and travel to the next province, Saskatchewan. At first the land is flat and black. As we cross the 800 miles (1,300 kilometers) of prairie, it gives way to more rolling, yellow-brown land, and beyond that to hills, with the snow-capped Rocky Mountains in the distance. We spin past town after town, each with its own towering grain elevator. Later, specially designed railway cars will take the wheat to distant cities for milling, or to ports for export. Canada is among the world's foremost exporters of wheat. With good reason, Saskatchewan has been called "the breadbasket of the world."

After we pass Regina, capital of Saskatchewan, we notice increasing numbers of cattle ranches mixed in among the wheat farms. Many of these ranches and farms are enormous. Here and there, we see oil rigs pumping "black gold" out of the depths below. Larger towns with colorful names like Moose Jaw, Swift Current, and Medicine Hat break our journey. A restaurant meal, a trip to a shopping plaza, perhaps a movie, allow us to meet townspeople or local farmers in town for the day.

*Golden wheat and black oil*
*— from the same Alberta soil.*

*Old-time chuckwagon races are one of the highlights of the Calgary Stampede.*

*Klondike Kate helps take Edmonton back to the 1890's gold rush during Klondike Days activities.*

The terrain becomes more hilly as we continue west through Alberta and into Calgary on the edge of the Rocky Mountain foothills. Calgary, a large modern city sometimes called "the Dallas of the North," has grown rapidly during the past 15 years. World oil and gas shortages promise to make this oil-rich and gas-rich area a world center of commerce and finance. Modern highrise towers have mushroomed, and suburbs have sprawled out in every direction.

Just a few hours drive west of Calgary, the Trans-Canada begins to climb into the foothills and through mountain passes. We are into forests again. We pass Banff National Park. Together with Jasper, its sister park to the north, it preserves a vast stretch of the Canadian Rockies from uncontrolled development. The beauty of these parks brings pleasure to countless tourists and nature lovers.

If we had time, we might drive 160 miles (260 kilometers) north from Calgary to Edmonton, Alberta's capital. Edmonton, like Calgary, is a prosperous city propelled by the wealth of Alberta's natural resources. But it somehow avoids the boomtown feel of Calgary. It seems older, better organized and more carefully planned. It has large parks with cross-country ski trails, and a downtown system of underground walkways to protect those who wish to avoid the fierce Edmonton winters.

The city is the southern tip of one of the world's most exciting and difficult driving experiences. After the Japanese attacked Pearl Harbor in December, 1941, there were fears that they might invade North America through Alaska. To protect Alaska and northern Canada, the Canadian and American military authorities built the Alaska Highway. Using Edmonton as the southern peg, engineers and construction crews pushed the road more than 1,500 miles (2,400 kilometers) over some of the most unyielding terrain on the continent.

It goes northwest across the Rocky Mountains into Dawson Creek in northeastern British Columbia, and onward through the Yukon, into Alaska.

When it was first completed, the road was largely unpaved. It was so rough that even big army trucks made the journey in convoys to avoid the ever-present danger of breaking down in the northern wilderness. Today, the highway is much improved. But it is still a long and difficult journey, especially in the winter.

We will leave the Alaska Highway for another visit when we have more time and supplies for the journey. Instead, we continue westward.

**British Columbia.** The Trans-Canada twists and turns through spectacular mountain scenery. Snow-capped peaks, some hidden in the clouds, are everywhere. We go through Kicking Horse Pass on the Continental Divide. On the border between Alberta and British Columbia, a sign explains that from the Continental Divide westward, all streams, lakes, and rivers drain into the Pacific Ocean. Eastward, they drain into Hudson Bay or the Atlantic Ocean.

*A moment of glory on the Bella Coola River.*

As we press westward, the mountains open onto a broad valley. It runs roughly 1,000 miles (1,600 kilometers) north and south through the Rocky Mountain chain. In this Rocky Mountain Trench, as it is called, melting snow from the mountains collects into streams. These join to become the headwaters of the Fraser River, or the Columbia.

Farther west, we pass lumbering and mining towns and travel through long tunnels blasted into the mountains. We drive past signs warning us to be alert for rocks or snowslides, and on through the Rogers Pass. We zig-zag down again, this time into the Okanagan valley. In this large, fertile valley, fruit orchards cover the terraced hillsides. Still farther westward, the highway twists back and forth through yet another mountain range. Finally, we move down onto the floor of the Fraser River valley, one of the richest farming areas of Canada. Ahead of us is the city of Vancouver, only a short distance north of the U.S. border.

Vancouver is a beautiful modern city of more than a million people. It is also Canada's largest west-coast port. Breathtaking scenery and a mild climate make it a desirable place to live. Vegetation is lush, fed by frequent rains. Vancouver gets so much rain, especially in the fall and winter seasons, that a local joke explains that people don't die in Vancouver, they rust. In summer, broad beaches within an easy walk of the downtown business area draw thousands to the shore, even office workers at lunch hour.

From Vancouver, we drive aboard a ferry for the long trip to Vancouver Island and Canada's most westerly city, Victoria. Capital of British Columbia, Victoria has a slightly milder climate than Vancouver, and far less rain. The climate is so mild that residents say the only reason they know it's winter is because they don't have to mow the lawn that week.

*B.C. Place, Vancouver's new domed stadium, blends in perfectly.*

Vancouver Island is a lush area of forest-covered mountains. Lumbering and salmon fishing abound. Many deep, sheltered harbors offer small fishing boats ready protection.

We cross the island on what was until recently an unpaved logging road. On the other side is the open Pacific at Long Beach. We are now as far west as we can drive in Canada.

But our trip is still not over. Most of what we saw till now lay near the Trans-Canada Highway. But what visit to Canada would be complete without touching the country's last frontier, the Arctic North?

**The Arctic North.** This is easier said than done. North of the western provinces lies the Yukon and the Northwest Territories. Their vastness is hard to believe. Together they cover more than 1,500,000 square miles (3,900,000 square kilometers), one-third of the Canadian land mass. From 60° latitude, they stretch northward across the Arctic Circle for more than 2,100 miles (3,400 kilometers) to the North Pole and Canada's border with the Soviet Union. This huge area is home to less than one percent of the Canadian population.

Because the Canadian Arctic is so enormous, it is almost impossible to generalize about its geography or climate. It varies from a far northern land of permanent ice and snow, to the Canadian tundra, a desolate and rocky region where grass, bush, and small trees grow. This slowly gives way to the more temperate southern areas. Here memories of bitter cold winters can be set aside during the short spring and pleasant summer, when daytime temperatures average 70°F (21°C). We eventually reach the treeline, where forests carpet immense expanses of territory.

In the North, the angle of the sun leaves daylight hours very short in winter months. During the summer, however, the opposite is true. In June, daylight lasts so long that this land can truly be called "the land of the midnight sun."

Here, the impact of urban life and modern technology is being felt more and more. What were once exclusively native communities now have new settlers from the south. New white settlements also attract native residents. For many native people, a quick hamburger, a soft drink, and french fries are now as likely to be part of their diet as they are for Canadians in the heavily populated south.

Native trappers still go to their winter trap lines in the bush. They trade their fur catch much as their fathers and forefathers did before them. But there, too, change has taken place. The snowmobile has replaced the dogsled, and the long isolation of the trap line is now broken by two-way radio communication. Some trappers even get to and from their more remote lines by airplane.

The vast majority of Canada's Inuit still live in the North. For them, too, modern goods and services from the south are having their impact. There are few Inuit children today who do not go to public school. Modern medical facilities are accessible by air ambulance.

Since we can make only one stop in the Arctic North, we decide to make it in the largest city in the Northwest Territories. That is the capital, Yellowknife. We drive back to Vancouver International Airport. From here our trip is by air. First we fly eastward, back across the Rockies to Edmonton. In Edmonton's modern airport we board a Pacific-Western Airline flight to Yellowknife. As our plane lands, we look out over the city. It hugs the north shore of Great Slave Lake, on a rough and stony terrain.

Neither the Northwest Territories nor the Yukon is a province. The federal government in Ottawa is responsible for them. However, both have local governments to care for most local matters.

*An agile participant in the Arctic Winter Games.*

Yellowknife is less than 300 miles (480 kilometers) from the Arctic Circle. With nearly 10,000 people, it is the largest town in the Northwest Territories. It contains modern facilities of every kind — from a hospital and schools to a radio and television center, modern shopping areas, and sports facilities.

Not all the sports are quite what we are used to. In winter, there is snowshoeing, snowmobiling, and dog-sledding, as well as skiing. In summer, camping and fishing are popular. During the longest day of the year, Yellowknife sponsors its annual Midnight Golf Tournament. Play begins at midnight. It will still be fully light for many hours.

Many of those who came to Yellowknife from southern Canada did not intend to stay permanently. They came to work temporarily for the government or in the gold mines, which have been a source of Yellowknife's wealth for almost 50 years. But many short-term employees fell in love with the northern way of life and made permanent homes there. Yellowknife's isolated location and harsh winter climate have bred a mood of informality and neighborliness among the townsfolk, so that few want to leave.

Our trans-Canada journey draws to a close. The many variations we found along the way in geography, climate, and vegetation provide but a taste of what Canada holds. But if our trip is over, our journey is only beginning. We did not stay in any one place long enough to develop a sense of how Canadians think, what they want for themselves and their land, what concerns they have for tomorrow. This will come from further study.

We have learned that there is no single correct picture of all Canada or all Canadians. Differences abound. Yet, as we will discover, there are ties that bind the people together. If Canadians defy all efforts to generalize about them, they do nevertheless make up a nation.

# Double-check

## Review

1. Name the three Canadian Prairie Provinces.

2. Why has Winnipeg been called "the gateway to the Canadian West"?

3. Why is the province of Saskatchewan called "the breadbasket of the world"?

4. Name the city that is Canada's largest western port.

5. Which region is considered Canada's last frontier?

## Discussion

1. "The West is the new economic force to be reckoned with in Canada today." Discuss this statement. Do you think the West's resentment of eastern Canada is justified? Explain your answer.

2. Why is oil called "black gold"? In what ways is oil used? Where else in the world can it be found? How have oil and gas shortages affected world economy and world politics in recent years? What has Canada's role been in these events?

3. The Yukon and the Northwest Territories are the two remaining territories belonging to Canada. What are the advantages to them of remaining territories? What are the disadvantages? Why do you suppose people move to the territories? Why might they stay there?

## Activities

1. The Canadian West has wonderful places to visit, such as Banff National Park, Jasper National Park, and Vancouver Island. Students might design brochures to advertise the tourist attractions of the Canadian West. They could use pictures from magazines or other sources, but should write their own copy.

2. The polar bear is one of many animals that can be found in the Canadian North. Students might want to get information about the animals found in Canada, or choose a specific animal for in-depth research. They could write a short, illustrated report.

3. An excellent author of Canadian wildlife stories is Farley Mowat. Some students might be interested in reading *Never Cry Wolf, The Polar Passion, Owls in the Family,* or *A Whale for the Killing,* and writing a book report.

# Skills

## TYPICAL YEARLY EXPORTS

millions
of dollars

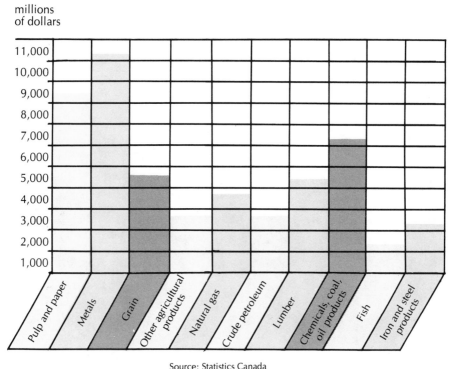

Source: Statistics Canada

*Use the bar graph above and information in Chapter 5 to answer the following questions.*

1. What do the bars on the graph represent?

2. By dollar value, what is Canada's largest export? What is its smallest?

3. What is the value of grain exported per year? Where is most of Canada's wheat grown?

4. What is the value of combined lumber and pulp and paper exports? Which province of Canada is especially rich in lumber resources?

5. What is an especially rich natural resource of the Yellowknife area of Canada's North? In which section of the graph would this resource be included?

3
EARLY
DAYS

# Chapter 6

# Natives, Explorers and Early Settlers

Just as they share a continent, the United States and Canada also share a history. The border that today separates Canada from the United States was not always there. Long before it was drawn, there was still the land. In both countries, prehistoric migrations established native communities thousands of years before the arrival of Europeans. The people who lived on the land were Indians and Inuit (Eskimos), today known as the native people.

**The original inhabitants.** It is believed that the native people originally migrated into North America more than 20,000 years ago. During the last Ice Age, Asia and North America were linked by an ice bridge across the Bering Strait. Gradually, nomadic people made their way across that bridge. They were probably following the migrating animals that supplied their food. Over many generations, these people spread and settled across the whole of North America and into South America.

Eskimaux men of igloolik, *from an 1824 engraving.*

With so many variations in climate, vegetation, game, and natural resources across the continent, differences in language, religion, and culture emerged. Native tribes, or bands, developed. Each carved out its own territory. Neighboring bands traded with one another. Sometimes they fought wars or joined in defensive alliances, just as the Europeans did.

**Viking adventurers.** We may never know exactly when Europeans first made contact with the native people. More than 1,000 years ago, Vikings from Scandinavia settled Iceland. They then moved into Greenland. Their folk sagas tell exciting tales of Viking adventurers who made their way still farther westward to a new land beyond the sea. Historians, however, have long tried to separate the fact of these sagas from the fiction. Archeologists have recently unearthed evidence of Viking landings in Newfoundland and Labrador.

One of the first verified landings in North America was by sailor Bjarni Herjulfson. He was reportedly driven off course as he sailed his tiny boat westward from Iceland to Greenland more than 500 years before Columbus set sail. Driven to the southwest by fierce winds, Herjulfson is believed to have taken shelter in a Newfoundland cove. He then sailed across to Labrador before finding his way back to Greenland. He told exciting stories of the rocky, forested land he visited.

Eventually other Viking adventurers set out to see this New World for themselves. Leif Ericson and his crew are said to have reached Newfoundland and Labrador in 995, almost 1,000 years ago. It is not known exactly where Ericson landed. Viking sagas suggest that it was a pleasant, grassy area with thick vegetation. His crew reported to have enjoyed the wild grapes they found growing along the coast so much that Ericson named the region Vineland. The adventurers loaded their boat with a cargo of timber, which they carried back to lumber-short Greenland.

Other Viking seamen followed. They, too, took back cargoes of timber and furs. A more permanent Viking settlement was probably attempted on the northeastern tip of Newfoundland, but it failed. The settlers and other Vikings doubtlessly made contact with the local native people. They would have traded with the natives and perhaps even fought with them, but details about the settlement or why it dissolved remain unclear. Eventually, Viking interest in the lands to the west died away. Again, we do not know why.

*Viking lore comes to life at the Icelandic Festival in Gimli, Manitoba.*

**The pathmakers.** Other Europeans may have known about the New World even before Columbus. Hearty European fishermen are believed to have sailed their small fishing craft to the rich fishing grounds off the Newfoundland coast. They likely hoped to keep those fishing grounds secret, to prevent others from sharing their catch.

Only after Christopher Columbus's famous voyages is the record clear. Columbus's dream of sailing west in search of the fabled Indies is well known. Like many of the explorers who followed, he did not realize at first that he had reached a new continent. He believed he was at the western edge of Asia.

Even as Spanish and Portuguese explorers and adventurers claimed much of the Caribbean and South America for their kings, they continued their hunt for an easy sea passage westward to the Indies. They thought at first that the new western lands were a large chain of islands. Until these lands were more fully explored, they could not know there was no sea route through them, from the north of what would be Canada to the southern tip of South America.

The English, French, and Dutch were jealous as the Spanish brought gold out of the Americas. They did not want to be denied the riches of the new lands or of the Indies all were sure lay just beyond. They, too, sent out explorers. They hoped to find a western sea route to the Indies, claim land for their own countries, and grow rich. Since the Spanish and Portuguese had already laid claim to the south, they were forced to concentrate their efforts to the north. This area would become the eastern United States, north of Florida.

**John Cabot.** Leading off for the English, in 1497, was the Italian-born sailor Giovanni Caboto, more commonly known as John Cabot. Like Columbus, Cabot was looking for the sea route to the Indies. On

Jacques Cartier

John Cabot

Henry Hudson

SHIPS OF THE TIME
OF CABOT AND
CARTIER

The Grand Hermine,
Cartier's largest ship
of 126 tons.

End of
the 15th Century.

the authority of British King Henry VII, and with the financial support of several English nobles, Cabot set sail. His small ship, the *Matthew,* carried a crew of only 18 men. Cabot made land, likely at Cape Breton in what is now Nova Scotia. He claimed it for the king of England. Mistakenly thinking he had reached the tip of the Indies, Cabot sailed southward in search of riches. He found no gold, silks, or spices. The onset of winter forced him back toward England. As he circled back, he passed the southern tip of Newfoundland and sailed through the Grand Banks. He reported that fish were so thick there that his crew scooped them out of the sea in a water bucket.

A second, larger voyage was organized the next year. Cabot was no more successful in discovering a westward passage to the Indies this time. Discouraged by his failure, his wealthy English backers refused to put up money for yet another voyage. It was his explorations, however, that allowed England's claim to Newfoundland and part of Nova Scotia.

**Jacques Cartier.** It was now France's turn to send out an explorer. A mapmaker and sailor named Jacques Cartier took on the task. Cartier had grown up near the sea, where he heard the stories of local fishermen. He was especially excited by their tales of a land far to the west surrounded by rich fishing grounds. In 1534, he sailed westward, supported by the French king, Francis I. He made his way around the north tip of Newfoundland and into the Gulf of St. Lawrence. On the south shore, he erected a large wooden cross and claimed all the surrounding lands in the name of Francis I. He also traded iron trinkets, pots, and knives with the local Indians for furs. With his cargo on board, he sailed as far as the wide mouth of the St. Lawrence River. He did not know this was a river and hoped it might be the sought-after western passage to the Indies.

Cartier's exciting report and his cargo of furs encouraged the king to raise the money necessary for a second and larger voyage of three ships. On this second trip, Cartier made his way up the St. Lawrence. Imagine his disappointment when the water turned from salt water to fresh. Fresh water meant he was on a river flowing from the interior, not on a direct salt-water passage connecting the Atlantic to the Pacific. Discouraged, Cartier nevertheless explored up-river as far as an Indian village called Hochelaga, the present site of Montreal. Here he again claimed all lands for France and traded with the Indians. This time, in addition to furs, he received a few nuggets of gold from local Indians.

Cartier and his men wintered on the icy banks of the St. Lawrence. They had never experienced such a cold and snowy winter. They also suffered many losses from scurvy. The survivors endured only with the help of the natives, who taught them how to make a medicinal brew from white cedar trees.

*Cartier meets the natives. 1535.*

Cartier was worried the French king would not support a third voyage. He had only a few nuggets of gold and furs to show for all the time and money his voyage had cost. To keep the royal court interested in a western passage, he kidnapped several Indians and took them back to France with him. These natives told the French stories of a great salt-water sea not far to the west. Perhaps they referred to Hudson Bay. The French, including Cartier, hoped the natives might lead them to a short overland route to the Pacific.

It was five years before Cartier returned to the New World. This time he had five ships and, for the first time, passengers. A small band of French settlers were on board. The French king hoped they could form a colony to tap the riches of the new world. Perhaps he dreamed the settlers would soon send cargoes of gold back to France, just as the Spanish were doing from their colonies farther to the south.

A small settlement was organized at Cap Rouge in 1541, near the present site of Quebec City. Unfortunately things did not go well. The colonists were less interested in establishing a colony than in getting rich quickly. Relations with the local Indians went from bad to worse. The settlers, instead of finding riches and a comfortable life, suffered hardship and disappointment. The metal and stones gathered at the river's edge proved to be neither gold nor diamonds. Dreams of instant wealth disappeared. The colony was soon abandoned. Cartier returned to France disappointed and died soon afterward.

**Henry Hudson.** The search for gold and a route to the Pacific continued in vain. In 1576, Martin Frobisher, from England, sailed northward in a fruitless effort to find a northern sea route to the east. He was followed, some years later, by Henry Hudson. Hudson had previously explored the Hudson River and the Delaware

Bay area for the Dutch. In 1610, he sailed north, this time under the British flag. He rounded the roof of the continent and sailed into a vast body of salt water, claiming the surrounding lands for the king of England. At first Hudson believed he had finally reached the Pacific. He was wrong. It was, instead, an enormous bay of salt water, an inland sea which now bears his name. By the time he discovered his error, it was too late in the autumn to sail back. He and his crew suffered a difficult winter on the shores of Hudson Bay. In the spring, when he insisted on continuing his exploration, his disheartened crew mutinied. Hudson and a few loyal crew members were cast adrift in a small boat. They were never heard from again.

All efforts to find gold or a sea route through the New World to the Indies failed. However, the explorers, through their impossible search, had opened up a new continent.

**Early settlers.** Explorers were gradually followed by traders and settlers. They, too, hoped to exploit the riches that might be found in the new world. In 1604, three years before the founding of Jamestown in Virginia and 16 years before the Pilgrims set foot on land at Plymouth, a small band of French settlers sailed into the Bay of Fundy. They landed first at St. Croix, but then moved the following year to Port Royal. Their agricultural colony, in what is now Nova Scotia, was called Acadia.

*The beginnings of a very early settlement.*

Champlain superintending the building of the Habitation of Port Royal, the 1st permanent settlement in North America.

Based on Champlain's engraving & on the reconstruction erected by the Dominion National Parks Bureau in 1939-40.

C.W. JEFFERYS

Acadia was soon joined by a second French colony in North America. In 1608, as Henry Hudson sailed in search of a sea route to the Indies, Samuel de Champlain arrived from France with a band of settlers. Champlain had been at Port Royal. This time he established the small colony of New France on the banks of the St. Lawrence River. That first settlement gradually grew to become present-day Quebec City.

72

**Royal charter.** New France was a French colony, but it was not ruled directly by the French king. For more than 50 years after the founding of Quebec, Henry IV of France did not send a governor to New France. Instead, he granted to a series of private trading companies a royal charter to operate in the colony. It guaranteed each company, in turn, an almost total monopoly to trade with the native people and govern the new colony.

Henry IV, of course, expected to be paid for his royal charter. Each company promised the French monarch a share in all company profits. In addition, it pledged to encourage the conversion of the native people to the Catholic faith, supervise the orderly settlement of French colonists on the land, enforce the king's laws, and defend the colony from attack.

Between the founding of Quebec in 1608, and 1663, when the royal charter was revoked, each company tried its hand at turning a profit in the New World.

*Indians trading furs.*

They had only modest success. The French continued to look with envy at the cargoes of gold being shipped back to Spain from the Spanish colonies to the south. No gold flowed out of New France.

There was profit to be made by trading in furs with the natives. But neither the native people nor the trading companies saw much benefit from encouraging French agricultural settlers to move into the young colony. The native people feared the Europeans would want their lands. The trading companies saw little profitable return from money spent on encouraging settlement. The money was in the fur trade. Thus, when the royal charter was revoked in 1663, there were only about 2,500 French people in the colony. A good number of these were fur traders, not farmers.

**Western exploration.** When a trading settlement was established at Quebec in 1608, Champlain was the colony's leader. He took command of every aspect of the settlement's growth. He enforced French law and organized the fur trade with the native people. He also encouraged the Catholic Church to carry its message to the native people.

But Champlain was not content to manage the colony from the Quebec settlement. He organized trading posts farther inland. One was the present site of Montreal. He still hoped to discover a passage to the Indies, with the help of the native people. He befriended the Huron Indians, who traded furs with the French. They soon allied themselves with the French against the Iroquois and the British. With his native allies, Champlain made several trips west to look for the fabled salt sea. In 1608 and 1609, he joined a war party against the Iroquois as it made its way into what is now central New York state. He reached a large lake, which now bears his name. There he and his Huron allies surprised and defeated an Iroquois war party.

*Running a rapid on the Mattawa River.*

In 1613, Champlain traveled the Ottawa River waterway by canoe. The route thereafter became a French shortcut into the western interior and a major route for bringing furs from the west to Quebec. In 1615, he also made his way to the Great Lakes. To his disappointment, he never found the western passage.

Even when old age and the demands of governing the colony kept him in the settlement, Champlain sent out other French explorers and adventurers. One was Jean Nicolet. In 1634, Nicolet set out, convinced he would reach the Indies. He went prepared. In his canoe he took special silk robes to wear when he was presented at the court of the Chinese Emperor.

Needless to say, neither Nicolet nor any of the others Champlain sent out reached China. They did, nevertheless, explore much of the continent's vast interior. They started trade relations with the native people and broke a path for others to follow.

The era of the royal charter was drawing to a close. By 1663, King Louis XIV saw little benefit to France in continuing it. He wanted more agricultural settlement in, and more direct control over, his North American colony. He revoked the charter and sent a royal governor to New France to represent him.

# Double-check

## Review

1. Name the two main groups of native people who first lived on the land that makes up Canada today.

2. Who were the first Europeans to land in Newfoundland and Labrador? How many years ago did they land there?

3. John Cabot's explorations allowed England to claim what territory?

4. Where and when was the first French settlement established in the new world?

5. What were Samuel de Champlain's three major accomplishments in New France?

## Discussion

1. In order to receive a royal charter from the king of France, a trading company had to promise to convert the natives to Catholicism. Why was that so important to him? Was missionary work as prevalent in the English colonies? Why or why not?

2. The first settlers at Cap Rouge were more interested in trade than in agriculture. Why do you think that settlement failed? Why were the settlements in Acadia and New France more successful?

3. Land claims by European explorers began on the east coast and gradually extended westward into the interior. How did this affect the development of Canada? What evidence of this east-to-west pattern still exists today?

## Activities

1. Students might want to design a timeline mural showing the presence of the native people, the explorers, and the early settlers in the new world.

2. Some students might find out more about the Viking explorers by researching recent archeological discoveries. One or two might give an oral report; others may want to add information not covered in the reports.

3. Some students might pretend to be one of the first settlers in Cap Rouge or Port Royal in New France. A diary entry could explain why they decided to come there, what they found on their arrival, and how they felt about being there.

# Skills

## WHAT'S IN A NAME?

The name Canada is supposed to derive from what the Indians kept yelling at discoverer Jacques Cartier as they pointed up river: "Kanata! Kanata!" meaning "Yonder are our wigwams!" There was another view which held that the Indians conversed with Portuguese fishermen drying the cod they had taken off the Grand Banks. This view suggested that the Indians were really saying "Aca nada" in Portuguese, meaning "There's nothing here." That story points to the heart of things. This is a nothing place. Nowheresville. And here is the trick of it. If you are nothing you may also be anything...

Scholar and former diplomat Douglas LePan has found the Canadian passport a useful image for all this. The little blue booklet stamped in gold is one of the world's more precious commodities. It is the passport most often used by those operating international rackets or spy systems. Its popularity lies not just in the fact one can travel almost anywhere with it, but in the fact that one can speak almost any language with almost any accent. One can be a member of almost any race, "English or French or Ukrainian or Polish or Chinese, and still be a Canadian. One can, in fact, be almost anyone and still be a Canadian. To be a Canadian is to have a passport to the whole world."

Source: *The Making of the Nation* by William Kilbourn, McClelland & Stewart, 1973 (adapted).

*Use the passage above and information in Chapter 6 to answer the following questions.*

**1.** This passage is from what type of book?
   (a) novel   (b) collection of poems   (c) history book

**2.** What does the word *Kanata* refer to?
   (a) a river   (b) wigwams   (c) codfish

**3.** Where is the term *Aca nada* supposed to have come from?
   (a) Indians speaking to fishermen from Portugal
   (b) notes made by Italian explorer John Cabot
   (c) conversations between Henry Hudson and his crew

**4.** What does the author probably mean when he calls Canada "a nothing place"?
   (a) Canada looks very small on a map of the world.
   (b) Canadians do not have a strong sense of peoplehood.
   (c) For traveling overseas, a Canadian needs a passport.

**5.** Why is it that "one can speak almost any language with almost any accent" and still be taken for a Canadian?
   (a) Everyone knows that most Canadians are excellent actors.
   (b) Canada shares borders with many countries of the world.
   (c) Canada's population is made up of people from many lands.

# Chapter 7

# *A Century of Conflict*

When Louis XIV revoked the royal charter and installed a royal government in the colony, one of the first tasks it took on was to encourage the growth of the French population. Jean Talon was made governor. He found less than 2,500 French settlers. Of these, only 1,000 were women. Talon encouraged both immigration from France and new births within the colony.

One of his more unusual steps was to import marriage-minded women from France to find husbands among the many bachelors. He fined bachelors who refused to wed, and encouraged French soldiers serving in New France to settle permanently in the colony on their discharge. He also offered cash bonuses to large families. In less than ten years, the population grew to more than 7,000 people.

There was never a large-scale immigration from France. Few landowners were willing to give up their peasants to populate distant Canada. Not even the king was prepared to allow too many of his subjects to move to the New World. What benefit could there be in depopulating his kingdom to populate Canada? If the population of New France was to grow, it would be through the encouragement of new births. And so it was. Just 100 years after Louis XIV took control of the colony, the population had grown from under 2,500 to almost 60,000.

**The seigneurial system.** The colonial government also tried to import the French feudal landholding system, the seigneurial system. Under it, a large tract of land was granted to a *seigneur.* As the landowner, he parcelled out smaller pieces to his tenants. Most of these small farms took the form of long narrow strips, often radiating up from a river's edge.

In return for the land grant, the seigneur pledged loyalty to the king and promised to help defend the kingdom from attack. He acted as judge in local disputes between his tenants, and supported the growth of the Church.

The tenants paid rent, offered the seigneur a portion of their harvest, worked the seigneur's personal lands, and served in the army if called. But a tenant was not like a peasant in France. The French peasants were downtrodden and tied by debt to their little pieces of land. The tenants in New France were not. Even though the population of New France grew, there was always a shortage of people. If a tenant felt mistreated by the seigneur, he might just pull up stakes and move on. What is more, New France was on the edge of a vast interior. If a tenant was not happy farming the land, there was always the lure of the land to the west.

Though the government, the Church, and the seigneurs tried to keep tenants on the land, many set out into the wilderness beyond the settlement. Money was always to be made in the fur trade. These free-spirited men, called *coureurs de bois* (runners in the woods), learned to live in the wilderness. Many took native wives. Although both the seigneurs and the Church frowned on their roaming way of life, these coureurs de bois became the backbone of the fur trade. And it was in the fur trade, more than in farming, that fortunes were to be made in New France.

*Fearless and self-reliant, the* coureurs de bois *roamed freely through New France.*

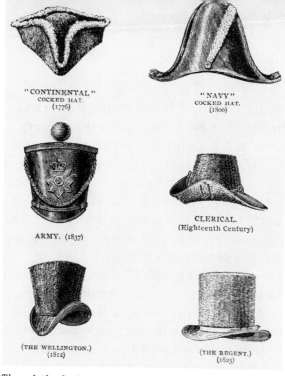

"CONTINENTAL"
COCKED HAT.
(1776)

"NAVY"
COCKED HAT.
(1800)

ARMY. (1837)

CLERICAL.
(Eighteenth Century)

(THE WELLINGTON.)
(1812)

(THE REGENT.)
(1825)

*Though the fashions changed, beaver hats remained popular for more than two centuries.*

**Competition for furs.** In Europe, beaver hats had become the fashion. As a result, the price for beaver pelts skyrocketed. In New France, trade with the Indians, especially for furs, became increasingly profitable. It was so profitable that others wanted a share. British merchants in the Thirteen Colonies joined the fur trade. They cared nothing for any monopoly granted by the French king. They jumped into the trade in competition with the French. Both groups were soon pushing inland in an effort to be closest to the native trappers.

After 1670, the fur merchants in both New France and the Thirteen Colonies had another competitor. That year, Charles II, King of England, awarded a royal charter of his own. He gave a newly formed English company exclusive trading rights in the lands claimed in his name by Henry Hudson. Perhaps thinking of the small rivers that gently flowed through the English countryside, Charles granted the Hudson's Bay Company control over all lands drained by rivers flowing into Hudson Bay. He did not know these rivers stretched all the way to the Continental Divide, more than 1,000 miles (1,600 kilometers) to the west. With the stroke of a pen, the company gained control of an enormous land mass. They named it Rupert's Land. It covered more than 1,000,000 square miles (2,600,000 square kilometers) of territory and was many times larger than England. It was also rich in furs.

Almost immediately, the Hudson's Bay Company fell into direct and often violent competition with the fur merchants in New France and the Thirteen Colonies. European demand for beaver pelts continued to grow. Competition stiffened and the beaver became scarce. Trappers were forced farther inland. Competing company agents followed them in their search for fur. Competing trading posts leap-frogged over one another into the interior of the continent.

Before long, much of the interior had been staked out. The French fur traders from New France claimed the St. Lawrence River valley, and the area around the Great Lakes and south through the Ohio and Mississippi River systems to the Gulf of Mexico. As the French pushed on, British merchants in the Thirteen Colonies found themselves hemmed in on the Atlantic. The French, for their part, felt squeezed between the heavily populated British colonies on the Atlantic and the powerful Hudson's Bay Company expanding out of the northwest. War threatened as trading block faced trading block.

**European wars enter the New World.** Friction between competing trading companies often threatened to become violent. Only a spark was needed to ignite frontier war. The spark was not long in coming. When Britain and France entered into war in Europe, their North American colonies soon became a battleground. Four times between 1689 and 1763, Britain and France sent troops against one another. Four times, the European conflict spilled over into North America. Four times, opposing camps in North America used the European conflict as a chance to grab land and influence from one another — often with the loss of many lives.

To make matters worse, long-standing feuds between native groups, especially the Iroquois and the Huron, broke into open conflict under cover of the European wars. The warring Iroquois and Hurons allied themselves with the opposing Europeans, the Hurons with the French and the Iroquois with the British. Once war broke out, the natives were supplied with arms by their European allies. They were encouraged to commit acts of violence against both natives and Europeans on the other side. For the natives, it was a way of settling scores of their own. Thus, wars brought on by disputes over the line of royal succession to the English, Spanish, or Austrian thrones left behind them trails of blood in North America.

**The Acadian expulsion.** The tragedy of war often echoes well beyond the roar of battle. In 1713, the British won the War of the Spanish Succession (known as Queen Anne's War in the North American colonies). Defeated, France was forced to hand over its colony of Acadia to the British. It was absorbed into the colony of Nova Scotia. But for the French settlers in Acadia, the change in power proved more than just simply trading a French king for a British one.

Under the British crown, the peaceful French Acadian farmers continued to live as a people apart. They were French speaking and Roman Catholic, and wanted to stay that way. The Acadians still outnumbered the British and other Protestant settlers in the surrounding region. Although they never took up arms against their new rulers, they refused to swear an oath of allegiance to the British crown. Mistrust grew. British

*Expelled Acadians*
*— sad victims of intolerance and greed.*

settlers feared the Acadians would rise up in support of France in the event of another war between the two countries. The Acadians were fearful for the future of their religion and language. From the New England colonies came repeated demands that the prosperous Acadian farmers be removed from their fertile land. These land-hungry British-American colonists wanted the Acadians out so they could take over the lands themselves.

In 1755, more than 40 years after the British took Acadia and more than 100 years after the Acadian settlement was first begun, approximately 11,000 Acadians were expelled from their homes. Some fled inland. Others moved north to resettle in New France. In the end, however, 6,000 Acadians were ruthlessly rounded up and deported. Families were often divided. Husbands and wives were sent to separate destinations, and children were lost to their parents. They were shipped to the southern-most American colonies and put ashore at various isolated locations. Some eventually found their way to then-French Louisiana. They helped stamp the Mississippi delta with the French character it has today. Years later, a small party made their way back to their lost settlement in Acadia. The Acadian tragedy shows the terrible power of intolerance and greed.

**The fall of Quebec.** In 1756, war again broke out in Europe between England and France. Once more the sounds of battle rumbled through North America. At the end of this war, the Seven Years' War (or the French and Indian War as it was known in the colonies), France would cease to be a colonial power in North America.

In June, 1759, the war reached the walls of Quebec. A British fleet with 7,000 infantrymen, grenadiers, and gunners under General James Wolfe sailed up the St. Lawrence. They took up positions to the east of Quebec City and on the south shore of the river, opposite the city. A siege and an unsuccessful assault failed to dislodge the French defenders led by Louis-Joseph, Marquis de Montcalm. Wolfe knew that if he did not break into the city quickly, the onset of winter could make a victory impossible. Without winter supplies, he would be forced to abandon his mission and retreat back to Nova Scotia.

*Today the Plains of Abraham lie peacefully overlooking Quebec City.*

On the night of September 13, Wolfe made a daring move. Under the cover of night, 4,500 British troops were secretly transported across the river in small boats. They scaled the cliffs towering above the shore and overran a French sentry outpost. Sunrise found the British troops drawn up in battle formation just beyond the city walls. The city was surrounded and the British now held the commanding high ground. In the ensuing battle on the Plains of Abraham, both Wolfe and Montcalm were mortally wounded. The battle and bombardment of the city continued for five days. Finally the exhausted French defenders surrendered.

**The expansion of British North America.** The surrender of Quebec in 1759 was a turning point in the history of North America. Four years later, in 1763, British and French negotiators finally met to draw up a peace treaty. The defeated French gave up all their colonies in North America, except for two tiny islands, St. Pierre and Miquelon off the south coast of Newfoundland. These islands, which France still holds, were granted so French fishermen would always have a safe harbor in the New World.

British North America had expanded. It now included the Hudson's Bay Company territory of Rupert's Land to the northwest, Quebec (the area north of the St. Lawrence and Great Lakes, also known as Canada), Nova Scotia, Newfoundland, the Thirteen Colonies on the Atlantic, and the great western territory stretching to the Mississippi River.

## HUDSON'S BAY TERRITORY

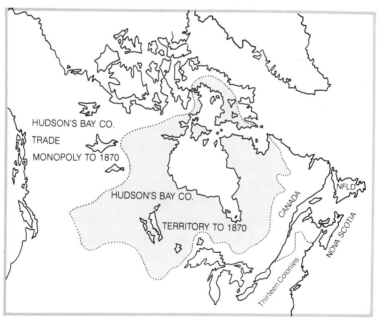

**Problems in the colonies.** Peace ended the rivalry between Britain and France. However, it did not bring harmony to British North America. Unfortunately for the British, whatever policy they considered for governing Quebec was bound to cause problems for them. It would either create revolt among the French or cause resentment in the Thirteen Colonies.

When the British acquired Canada, they inherited about 60,000 French-speaking Catholics. In the peace treaty, Britain guaranteed that these people need not give up their lands or their religion. There would be no Acadian-like expulsion. But what would be their status? Under British law, Roman Catholics could not vote, nor could they hold public office. Would these French Catholics have a voice in how they were governed?

Shortly after the British victory, about 600 English merchants, mostly from the Thirteen Colonies to the south, moved into what had been New France. They demanded an elected assembly like the one they had known. But they rejected any suggestion that the French Catholics should also have the vote. The British governor knew that if the French could not vote, control over the whole colony and its 60,000 population would fall into the hands of the 600 English newcomers. The result might spark a major French revolt. He refused to hold elections.

The British merchants protested to London. They wanted an assembly. They were supported in this by friends in the Thirteen Colonies. These people feared that if the British could refuse to establish an elected assembly in Canada, they might someday abolish assemblies in all the colonies.

The Thirteen Colonies had another reason to be angry with the British. They were upset about native lands. Until the fall of New France, many natives had been allies of the French. The Indians felt their lands were not threatened by French settlers. The French had been interested in trade, not land settlement. The British were different. The colonists wanted to expand settlement westward into Indian territory. The natives feared the British might open the interior to settlers from the Thirteen Colonies. The settlers did pressure the British government to open all lands to the Mississippi, but they refused. They wanted to avoid warfare with the natives just as they wanted to avoid revolt among the French. As a result, western lands were closed to settlement. The colonists were furious. To them, it seemed that the British government was treating old enemies (the French Catholics and the natives) better than loyal British colonists.

They soon had yet another reason to be angry. The British moved 10,000 troops into the Thirteen Colonies. They were to guard against another war and to prevent any illegal settlement of Indian lands. When taxes were laid on the colonists to pay for the troops, the cry of "No taxation without representation" was heard. The stage was set for the American Revolution.

**Canada and the American Revolution.** The story of the American Revolution and the birth of the United States is common knowledge. The important impact of the American Revolution on the growth and development of Canada is not as well known.

When revolution broke out in the Thirteen Colonies in 1775, the revolutionary forces hoped to capture Canada and make allies of its people. They were disappointed. Some colonists in Nova Scotia sympathized with the revolutionaries. But Nova Scotia was too dependent on British trade and commerce to join in the revolt. That was especially true around Halifax. Here a big British naval base ensured the town's prosperity and loyalty.

The French Canadians had little love for the British conquerors. They had even less trust of the Americans. After all, merchants from the Thirteen Colonies had tried to grab power after the British conquest of Canada. The revolutionaries were also thought to be anti-Catholic. The British governors, on the other hand, respected French language, customs, property, and religion. Thus, French Canadians and their church remained quietly neutral. It was, however, a neutrality that tilted a little to the British side.

**The invasion of Canada.** In June 1775, in the midst of the American Revolution, Congress approved an invasion of Canada. In August, the campaign was launched. General Richard Montgomery led an American force slowly north across New York, along a route pioneered by French fur traders almost 150 years earlier. In November 1775, they overwhelmed the small British garrison at Montreal. The British retreated into Quebec City and Montgomery laid plans for a siege.

Meanwhile, a second American force under Benedict Arnold marched overland through Maine. As winter set in, Arnold's men pushed on across Nova Scotia to join Montgomery outside the walls of Quebec City. Like Wolfe in 1759, Montgomery and Arnold had to act quickly or find their invasion plans stalled by the harsh winter. With the surrounding French Canadians neutral, the combined American force under Montgomery and Arnold finally organized an assault. On the last day of 1775, the cold and poorly armed Americans attacked. The attack failed. The British troops inside the walled city fought off the assault and captured 400 Americans. Montgomery was killed, and Arnold was wounded. The American force retired. It lay seige to Quebec City for the rest of the winter. But the toll on the Americans outside the city was far greater than it was on the warm and comfortable British defenders inside the walls.

*The seige of Quebec.*

In the spring of 1776, a British fleet with fresh troops and supplies sailed up the St. Lawrence to relieve Quebec. The bedraggled American troops, short on supplies and suffering from disease, retreated southward. The invasion of Canada was over.

**Peace.** Canada was not conquered during the American Revolution. However, Britain was defeated in the Thirteen Colonies. In 1781, British General Cornwallis surrendered his forces at Yorktown. The British government faced the inevitable. In 1783, it signed the Treaty of Versailles. Britain admitted defeat and recognized the new United States of America.

Britain also made a generous land settlement with its former colonies. Lands south of the Great Lakes and previously part of New France were given to the new republic. But lands to the north of the Great Lakes, the St. Lawrence valley, and Nova Scotia remained in British hands. A line was drawn. To the south was the United States. To the north was British North America.

# Double-check

## Review

1. Name the French king who set up a royal government in the French colony.

2. Explain who the *coureurs de bois* were.

3. Name the English company that was given exclusive trading rights in Rupert's Land by King Charles II of England.

4. After which war was France forced to give Acadia to the British?

5. What happened to the French colonies after the Battle of the Plains of Abraham?

## Discussion

1. What was the seigneurial system of land ownership in the French colonies? Why did some tenants stay to work the land? Why did others risk going to an unknown life in the wilderness? What would you have done?

2. Was killing animals for their fur a necessity in the French colonies or simply a profitable business? Was it the same as raising minks for their fur today? Explain your answer.

3. Although they were defeated at the Plains of Abraham, the French did not have to give up their land or their religion. What lesson had the British learned from their expulsion of the Acadians? Were their concessions to the French enough? Too much? Explain.

## Activities

1. Some students may enjoy the poem "Evangeline," which tells the story of two lovers expelled from Acadia. Others may be interested in finding out more about the "Cajuns," the descendants of the Acadians sent to Louisiana, as well as about where that name originated. A map of Louisiana will show many places with French names.

2. Some students might write a short biography of Louis-Joseph, Marquis de Montcalm, or of General James Wolfe, the opposing leaders in the Battle of the Plains of Abraham.

3. Students might write a letter from a British merchant who moved to New France after it became part of British North America, complaining to the governor that the British government is treating "old enemies" better than loyal British colonists. They should give specific reasons for the merchant's anger.

# Skills

## LETTER FROM A YOUNG PIONEER

*Atlantic Ocean, off the coast of France July 2, 1665*

My dear brother Stefan,

We had to wait two days for a favorable wind, but this morning the captain finally gave the order and we set sail.

I think that I will enjoy my voyage across the Atlantic. However, at this moment I am having a few anxious thoughts. I am wondering what sort of life awaits me in New France. You know that I sometimes felt restless and unhappy at the orphanage in Paris. Still, it was my home. Now I have left it behind forever!

But surely everything will be all right, don't you think? After all, it was our parish priest himself who asked me to volunteer. New France is still a weak colony, he said, even though it is over fifty years old. It doesn't have enough inhabitants to protect itself against the unfriendly Indians, or the colonists to the south. French girls of good character are needed to marry the bachelors of New France, to establish new homes and raise large families to increase the population.

I don't really know why I agreed to go. Perhaps it's because I want to do something for my country. Perhaps it is simply because I long for adventure and romance. Our Mother Superior and the Sisters at the orphanage certainly encouraged me. "You are a strong healthy girl," they said. "You will make a good pioneer."

So here I am, Stefan, bound for the new world. I hope that you are still happy staying with Monsieur and Madame Pierron. Do they make you work very hard in the sawmill? Please give my best regards to them.

Your loving sister,
Jeanne-Louise

Source: *Fish and Ships* by Elma Schemenauer, Globe/Modern Curriculum Press, 1981 (adapted).

*Use the letter above and information in Chapter 7 to answer the following questions.*

1. When did Jeanne-Louise write this letter?

2. Why were marriage-minded women encouraged to go to New France?

3. What enemies did New France have at the time?

4. How did Jeanne-Louise feel about becoming a pioneer?

5. The Roman Catholic Church played a big part in establishing and building up the colonies of New France. What references to this are there in the letter?

# Chapter 8

# From Colony to Confederation

Not only did the American Revolution result in the creation of the United States. In many ways, it eventually led to the creation of a second country. During the war, many thousands of American colonists had not supported the Revolution. Some fought on the side of the British army. These Loyalists, as they were called, now suffered at the hands of the American victors. In spite of guarantees that they would not be punished, many Loyalists had their lands and property taken away. Physical attacks and even tarring and feathering were common.

**The Loyalists flee north.** As a result, many Loyalists were forced to flee. They abandoned their homes to find refuge and build new lives under the protection of the

94

British crown. Fifty thousand settled just across the new border, along the north side of Lake Ontario and Lake Erie. Another 30,000 moved into western Nova Scotia. Smaller numbers went to other parts of British North America.

The British did what they could to prepare for the influx of Loyalists. But when so many arrived at one time, hardship could not be avoided. They soon swelled the local communities beyond anything that had been expected. In Nova Scotia, the population had been concentrated on the Atlantic seaboard. The Loyalists flooded into the western portion of the colony, far from Halifax. To better govern the region, the colony was divided into two, Nova Scotia to the east and New Brunswick to the west.

The area stretching along the St. Lawrence valley and north of the Great Lakes, then called Canada, also had problems. The Loyalist settlement split that colony. French-speaking Catholics lived along most of the St. Lawrence River valley. The English-speaking Protestant Loyalists settled westward along the shores of the Great Lakes. Each was suspicious of the other. How could a colony be governed with justice and security for both groups?

In 1791, the British parliament passed the Canada Act. Canada was divided into two colonies at the Ottawa River, Upper Canada (Ontario) and Lower Canada (Quebec). French and English centers of population were separated from one another. The French Catholics were granted the right to vote for an assembly. Traditional French civil law and the seigneurial land system was allowed to continue in Lower Canada.

The governor of Upper Canada invited additional settlers from the United States to live under the British flag. These "late Loyalists" swelled the new colony's population even further. But would they be loyal to the crown? The governor would soon find out.

**The War of 1812.** In 1812, Britain was at war with Napoleon of France. British warships repeatedly stopped American merchant vessels on the high seas. The British forcefully removed sailors who, they claimed, had earlier deserted from British ships. When they refused to stop these boardings, the United States threatened war.

Some people in the United States were pleased with the prospect of war with Britain. Western members of Congress formed a group known as the War Hawks. They had long wanted such a war as a pretext for an invasion of British North America. They hoped to annex Canada to the United States. With Britain occupied by a war in Europe, they figured Canada would fall like a ripe apple. The War Hawks also suspected that the British from Canada were stirring up the native people in the American West by supplying them with guns and ammunition. The British, they argued, still harbored hopes of retaking the United States. Keeping the American frontier alive with native unrest was part of the British plan.

On June 1, 1812, Congress declared war on Britain. The United States did not have the power to attack Britain on the other side of the Atlantic. But it could attack Canada. With a population of eight million, the United States was confident it could easily conquer Canada with its half-million people.

There were those in the United States who opposed the war, especially in the New England states. Their prosperity depended on trade with Britain. But an army to invade Canada was quickly raised. A proclamation was also issued calling upon Canadians to look upon the invaders as liberators.

In Canada, the military situation was grim. With Britain preoccupied by a war with France, there were only 4,500 British troops available to defend all of British North America from the larger and stronger

*D-Day, 1812. The British invade Detroit, under General Isaac Brock.*

American force. And the British were not sure whether the native people, the late Loyalists, and the French Canadians would be loyal to the crown.

Few Canadians looked at the Americans as liberators. Instead, they rallied under the Union Jack (the British flag). With their native allies, led by Chief Tecumseh, they took the offensive. Before the American army could attack, British forces crossed the border to defeat larger U.S. forces in several battles. In an effort to regain momentum, an American force struck north of the border at Queenston Heights, near Niagara Falls, in October, 1812. In a hard-fought battle, the U.S. force was finally defeated by British regulars and Canadian volunteers.

The War of 1812 is misnamed. It dragged on for several more years. In 1813, Americans crossed Lake Ontario and captured the small town of York (now Toronto), the capital of Upper Canada. They burned public buildings and destroyed British naval supplies before they moved on.

In August, 1814, the British and Canadians evened the score. They attacked Washington, the new United States capital. British troops burned public buildings, including the president's new home. This home was later repaired and the burn marks were covered with white paint. As a result, thanks to Canadians, the president's home became known as the White House.

The war ended in a draw. When Britain finally defeated Napoleon, it could have turned its full might against the United States. Wisely, war-weary American and British governments preferred the road to peace. In the Treaty of Ghent, signed on Christmas eve, 1814, the United States and Britain agreed to end hostilities. In 1817, the Rush-Bagot Treaty was signed. Both countries agreed to resolve all future differences through negotiations.

Word that a truce had been signed at Ghent did not reach North America for several weeks. Because of the delay, the biggest battle of the war was fought after it was already over. In early January, 1815, a powerful British force attacked New Orleans. A much smaller American force under General Andrew Jackson handed the British a crushing and unnecessary defeat, with the loss of many lives.

The War of 1812 marked a new beginning for North America. After peace was re-established, Canada and the United States never went to war with one another again. There have been disputes and talk of war over the years. But war has always been avoided.

**Rebellions in Canada.** The war had developed national spirit in British North America. Defending the colonies against an invader had created mutual pride. But pride in banding together to defend their land against the United States was one thing. That did not mean Canadians agreed about how they should be governed. Bitter disagreements eventually led them to take up arms against each other.

When the Loyalists had fled northward, they hoped to build a society that they and their heirs would rule. In Upper Canada, a small group of wealthy merchants came to dominate the agricultural colony. They were called the Family Compact, because they acted like a family and excluded everyone else. They controlled the assembly. They favored one another with jobs. Their church, the Church of England, was favored with land grants and other privileges. The Family Compact claimed to be more loyal to the crown than anyone else, and branded all those who opposed them as traitors. They rejected any move for reform.

*Rebel leaders: William Lyon Mackenzie (left) and Louis Joseph Papineau (right).*

In Lower Canada, a similar English-speaking ruling group was called the Chateau Clique. The Chateau Clique did not control the assembly, but they had great influence with the governor. They proposed the merger of Upper and Lower Canada. This would deprive French Canadians of the majority they held in Lower Canada's assembly. They also called for an end to French language rights in any united assembly. When the governor of Upper Canada seemed ready to back the Chateau Clique, French-Canadian protests began.

In 1837, protests in both Upper and Lower Canada boiled over. Separate rebellions broke out in the two colonies. Even though the uprisings were not united, they ran the same course. Rebel leaders, Louis Joseph Papineau in Lower Canada and William Lyon Mackenzie in Upper Canada, rallied their supporters for battle. Some took up arms. Others, including some who agreed with the cause of Papineau and Mackenzie, rejected armed rebellion. They feared rebellion would be a sure step toward an eventual takeover by the United States. In the end, the rebels were too weak and disorganized to defeat the government supporters aided by British regular troops. Papineau and Mackenzie fled to the United States. Many of their supporters were tried. Some were hung.

**The Durham Report.** Despite defeat, the rebellions had some influence on the future. The British realized that reform was needed. Otherwise violence would erupt again. They did not want another revolution. Lord Durham, a British aristocrat, was sent to investigate. He was a friend of reform, with a strong faith in democracy.

Durham's report recommended sweeping changes in the way Canada was governed. First, he wanted conflict between English and French to end. As he explained, "I expected to find a contest between a government and a

*ch or poor, the rebels of 1837 marched*
*ward the same fate.*

*Lord Durham*

people; I found two nations warring in the bosom of a single state." To end the warring, he called for the union of Upper and Lower Canada. This would be the first step toward the blending of the French into the majority English culture. If French culture disappeared, Durham believed, there would be no English-French conflict.

He also advocated democratic, responsible government. The British-appointed governor had the power to appoint a ruling council and could override the assembly. Instead, Durham wanted an elected assembly with powers to make laws on local matters. The leader of the largest political party would become the prime minister. He would choose his cabinet, or ruling council, from other elected members of the assembly.

Durham's recommendations were slow to be adopted. The merger between Upper and Lower Canada was approved in 1841, but not without opposition. French Canadians feared the merger would destroy their majority in Lower Canada. As a concession to them, the French language was eventually made equal to English in the united colony's assembly. Other concessions were also made. In important areas such as justice and education, there would be a separate administration for French Canada in the east and English Canada in the west. Thus, French language and culture were secured. Durham's hope that the French would be assimilated was ignored.

**Responsible government.** Responsible government came to Canada only after it had been won in the neighboring British colony of Nova Scotia. There, a reform newspaperman and politician, Joseph Howe, challenged the Council of Twelve, the local version of the Family Compact. He led the Nova Scotia assembly in demanding responsible government. He wrote the British government: "We seek nothing more than British subjects are entitled to; but will be content with

*Joseph Howe addresses an open-air meeting.*

nothing less." In 1846, Howe won. The governor of Nova Scotia was obliged to choose his council from the party with the most seats in the assembly. What is more, it was soon almost unthinkable for the governor to reject their advice.

Responsible government finally came to a merged Canada as well. The old Family Compact and the Chateau Clique lost their preferred positions. A year later, they showed their contempt for the democratic process. A reform-minded majority had been elected to the assembly. Many of these reformers thought of the 1837 rebels not as traitors but as pioneers in the struggle for responsible government. The assembly passed a controversial act, the Rebellion Losses Act, to compensate those who had fought on both sides in the rebellion for property loss. Those who opposed the bill protested that those who had supported the rebellion should not receive compensation, since they had been traitors.

The governor personally opposed the bill. He was also urged by the minority not to sign it into law. Bowing to the will of the majority, however, he did sign. As he rode to the parliament building to sign the bill, he was booed by an unruly and hostile crowd. When he emerged after signing it, he was pelted with stones and eggs.

The crowd grew uglier. The governor escaped with the aid of armed cavalry. The mob then stormed into the parliament building. Gas jets used to light and heat the building were ripped from the walls. Gas soon filled the air and an explosion ripped through the building. As it burned, the mob prevented the fire brigade from reaching it.

After several days of disorder, cooler heads prevailed. The rioters were condemned. The law stood. The democratic will of the elected assembly was supreme, even over the governor. Responsible government was victorious.

**Pressures for political union.** Even with representative government firmly in place, British North America was still disunited and economically weak. Compared with the great influence and growing industrial might of the United States, economic growth in British North America was painfully slow. Each of the colonies remained separate and distinct from the others. They competed with one another for British and American markets in which to sell their products. Their populations were too small to create a healthy local market. To make matters worse, transportation along railways, roads, and canals was not nearly good enough to ensure common economic growth or defense. Difficulties between the English and French also continued.

And always there was the lingering suspicion of American intentions. Many in Canada remained convinced that the United States still wanted to annex British North America, maybe even by force. It had failed to conquer the colonies in the War of 1812, but it was now stronger and more self-assured.

In the 1860's, fear of a U.S. invasion of British North America spread. During the bloody American Civil War, the Union was angered by alleged British support for the Confederacy. Some Americans called for an invasion of Canada.

When the Civil War ended in 1865, tension with the United States grew worse. Hundreds of discharged U.S. soldiers, many originally from Ireland, joined a military society called the Fenians. The Fenians wanted to force Britain out of Ireland. But since an attack on Britain was impossible, they trained openly for one on British North America.

The U.S. government did not officially approve of the Fenians. But it also did nothing to stop their recruiting and military preparations. In 1866, Fenians raided across the border near Niagara and along the New Brunswick frontier. They were driven back without trouble. Today, the Fenian attacks may seem like something out of a comic opera, but at the time they seemed a very real threat to British North America.

**Confederation.** How could British North America cope with the internal problems? How could the separate colonies defend themselves against the American threat? How could they finance better transportation, promote stronger economic growth, and ease English-French disputes?

Unlike the United States, Canada did not win its self-government on bloodstained battlefields. Canadians did not rise up in rebellion against the British. Rather, their political leaders, with British government encouragement, negotiated among themselves to establish a political union of the British North American colonies, and the terms of its government. Each of the colonies had its own interests to protect. None wanted

*The Fathers of Confederation.*

to lose economically. French-speaking Canadians were concerned for their language rights. Catholics wanted guarantees for their religious rights and public funding of Catholic schools. Local politicians demanded that their powers to run local affairs not be taken away by a new federal government.

Compromise was not easy. While the Union and the Confederacy in the United States battled to decide on the future of their republic, arguments for and against a political union of the British colonies raged on. Debate seemed endless. Some opposed giving up any local powers to a central government. Others saw little benefit for themselves in a united country. The Fenian threat finally gave a boost to the unity side. A united British North America was necessary.

In the end, hopes for future economic growth and fear of American designs won the day. A confederation agreement was hammered out. Once endorsed by local legislatures, it went to the British parliament to be passed into law. The British were pleased to see an end to the squabbling among its colonies in North America. They also hoped the new confederation could pay more of its own defense bill. Parliament in London quickly passed the British North America Act that created Canada.

The colonies were officially united into one country on July 1, 1867. The British North America Act established Canada as a confederation of four provinces — Nova Scotia, New Brunswick, Quebec (Lower Canada), and Ontario (Upper Canada). Each province had its own assembly and powers. However, national powers rested with the central government. Not all the colonies immediately joined Confederation, as it was called. Prince Edward Island waited until 1873, and Newfoundland, the first British colony in North America, remained separate from Canada until 1949.

To the north and west of the new Canada stretched Rupert's Land, still in the hands of the Hudson's Bay Company. Across the Rocky Mountains was a small and isolated British colony in British Columbia. And to the south was the powerful United States.

Ahead lay a challenge. Would Canada survive and grow? In the years that followed, Canadians would bridge a continent from the Atlantic to the Pacific. They would gradually and peacefully assert full independence from Britain. They would wrestle with internal divisions. And as they did this, they would build a pride in their identification as Canadians.

*The British North America Act was as important to Canada as the Constitution is to the United States.*

### BY THE QUEEN.
# A PROCLAMATION
### For Uniting the Provinces of Canada, Nova Scotia, and New Brunswick into One Dominion under the Name of CANADA.

VICTORIA R.

WHEREAS by an Act of Parliament passed on the Twenty-ninth Day of March One thousand eight hundred and sixty-seven, in the Thirtieth Year of Our Reign, intituled " An Act for the Union of Canada, Nova Scotia, and New Brunswick, and the " Government thereof, and for Purposes connected therewith," after divers Recitals, it is enacted, that " it shall be lawful for the Queen, by and with the Advice of Her Majesty's most Honorable " Privy Council, to declare by Proclamation that on and after a Day therein appointed, not being " more than Six Months after the passing of this Act, the Provinces of Canada, Nova Scotia, and " New Brunswick shall form and be One Dominion under the Name of Canada, and on and after " that Day those Three Provinces shall form and be One Dominion under that Name accordingly:" And it is thereby further enacted, that " such Persons shall be first summoned to the Senate as " the Queen, by Warrant under Her Majesty's Royal Sign Manual, thinks fit to approve, and " their Names shall be inserted in the Queen's Proclamation of Union:" We therefore, by and with the Advice of Our Privy Council, have thought fit to issue this Our Royal Proclamation, and We do Ordain, Declare, and Command, that on and after the First Day of July One thousand eight hundred and sixty-seven the Provinces of Canada, Nova Scotia, and New Brunswick shall form and be One Dominion under the Name of Canada. And We do further Ordain and Declare, that the Persons whose Names are herein inserted and set forth are the Persons of whom We have, by Warrant under Our Royal Sign Manual, thought fit to approve as the Persons who

# Double-check

## Review

1. Who were the Loyalists?

2. What did the Canada Act do?

3. Who were the War Hawks?

4. What was the Family Compact?

5. What important event occurred on July 1, 1867?

## Discussion

1. In 1817, the United States and Britain signed the Rush-Bagot Treaty, agreeing to resolve future problems through negotiation rather than through war. What difference would this make in later events involving the two countries? What might make it difficult to carry out such a treaty?

2. In his report, Lord Durham suggested responsible government for British North America. What does "responsible government" mean? Name some countries of the world that do not have responsible government today.

3. Canada became a nation in 1867, through negotiation rather than through violence. Why was the situation in Canada different from that in the Thirteen Colonies in 1776?

## Activities

1. Chief Tecumseh, who fought bravely alongside the British during the War of 1812, attempted to form a confederacy of tribes to protect Indian land from American expansion. A group of students might find Canadian author Charles Mair's verse-drama *Tecumseh* and do an oral reading for the class.

2. Pairs of students might research and present one of the "Fathers of Confederation" to the class, telling who he was, where he was from, and what his interests were. Some pairs might want to use an "interview" presentation, live or taped.

3. Canada Day, July 1, which marks the birthday of Canada's Confederation, is celebrated in much the same way as July 4 is in the United States. The class might plan a Canada Day celebration with Canadian music, posters, books, magazines, etc. Typically Canadian foods, some Quebec or Newfoundland step dances, and clothes of the period would add interest.

# Skills

## LIFE IN LOYALIST NEW BRUNSWICK

GARDEN SEEDS
ROBERT REID
Has just received an assortment of fresh *Garden Seeds* of last year's growth, which he offers for Sale on reasonable terms at his shop in King Street.

IMPORTED
In the Brig Susannah, John Watt, Master, from Liverpool, and for Sale by Daniel King
Liverpool Salt,
Ale in barrels,
Soap and Candles
A few Table and Tea Sets of Liverpool China,
Also, a compleat assortment of Earthen Ware in crates and hhds.
Stone bottles from 2½ to 5 gallons
He Has Also on Hand
Sugar in barrels,
Rum and Molasses.

A dentist's advertisement:
"...tooth and gum brushes, chew sticks, tinctures, and dentifrices adapted to the several ages and complaints and suited to both warm and cold climates. For sale by retail or by the quantity with directions for their use."
He also offered to make loose teeth firm, harden gums, repair damaged teeth, and stretch a too-crowded jaw "without PAIN."

Advertisement in the *Royal Gazette*, 1836:

"Wanted — An apprentice to the Painting Business — a boy about 14 years of age. One from the country and a member of the Temperance Society would be preferred. Apply to Charles P. Smiler

Source: *New Brunswick: The Story of Our Province* by MacBeath and Chamberlin, Gage, 1965.

*Use the above advertisements and information in Chapter 8 to answer the following questions.*

1. What were some of the occupations you would find among New Brunswick Loyalists?

2. What is an *apprentice*? What sort of person was Charles P. Smiler looking for as an apprentice?

3. Where had the goods come from that were described in the advertisement beginning *IMPORTED*?

4. Where did the New Brunswick Loyalists come from? Why?

5. In what other areas of British North America besides New Brunswick did the Loyalists settle?

# 4
# STILL
# GROWING

# Chapter 9

# A New Country
# in the New World

The British North America Act of 1867 spelled out the form, powers, and responsibilities of the federal and provincial governments in Canada. It also reaffirmed that, although Canada was now self-governing, it remained under the British crown. Canadians were British subjects. Queen Victoria was still their Queen.

Canada was linked to Britain in two important areas. First, revisions in the Articles of Confederation, by which the country was governed, still had to be approved by the parliament in London. This was seldom a problem. But it eventually became embarrassing for an independent, self-governing country to have to ask approval of another parliament for amendments to its government structure. Secondly, Britain officially represented Canada in all foreign affairs and in negotiating international agreements.

Initially, few Canadians objected to the continuation of these ties. They were proud of their British connections. Canada might be self-governing, but most Canadians still saw themselves as defenders of the British way of life in North America and a partner in the British Empire. Yet, the confederation of provinces to form Canada did represent an important move. It was a giant step toward nationhood. If Canada was not yet fully independent of Britain, it was also no longer a colony. A new country had come into being.

**Expansion to the west.** Canada has as its motto the Latin phrase *A Mari Usque ad Mare.* This means "From sea to sea." Such a grand phrase must surely have sounded foolish in 1867, when Canada's new parliament met for the first time in Ottawa. The new country was a far cry from the Canada of today. At the time, it was made up of only four provinces. The whole country lay nestled along the north Atlantic coast, the north shore of the lower Great Lakes, and the St. Lawrence River. This was hardly "from sea to sea."

However, Canada's first prime minister, John A. Macdonald, had a grand dream for the future of the country. He made westward expansion a priority. Only two years after Confederation, in 1869, Macdonald negotiated a Canadian takeover of Rupert's Land. That area had been governed by the Hudson's Bay Company under a royal charter granted in 1670. It was eight times larger than the existing area of Canada, and larger than today's United States and Mexico combined.

The British government and the Hudson's Bay Company had become concerned about the territory's future, A growing population in the western United States threatened to spill north into Rupert's Land. If this "peaceful invasion" took place, it was feared that American annexation might follow. Both the company and Britain preferred to see it become part of Canada.

With the approval of the British government, the company officially gave control of Rupert's Land to Canada. In return, it retained the right to trade in the area, and ownership of the land surrounding its trading posts. It also received large grants of land it might resell later, and a cash payment of $1,500,000. For Canada, this was a very small price for almost half a continent. Overnight, the young country became one of the world's largest.

*Sir John A. Macdonald, Canada's first prime minister, retained his dream of a country stretching "from sea to sea."*

*Early days in the Red River Colony.*

**The Red River Rebellion.** This new territory was later named the Northwest Territories. It was largely empty of Europeans. The only important settlement was the Red River Colony just north of the Wisconsin border. This colony had no direct overland transportation links with the rest of Canada. Travel west across the Canadian Shield to the newly acquired territories was difficult. Travelers had to make their way through the United States and enter the Northwest Territories from the south.

Before Canada could officially absorb the area, trouble was already brewing. The Red River settlers were squabbling among themselves. Some welcomed the union with Canada. Others saw economic advantages in union with the nearby United States. The largest group, the Métis, distrusted both Canada and the United States.

Almost 10,000 of the colony's 12,000 population were Métis. They were descendants of native people and European fur traders. For the most part, they were also French speaking and Roman Catholic. They resented not being consulted about the future of the Red River

Colony. What would the Canadian takeover mean to them? Would it threaten their French language and Catholic religion? They lacked official titles to their lands, and the Métis asked the government for guarantees that those lands would not be taken away when Canadian authorities moved in. They received no reply from Ottawa.

Their unease grew. The Métis prevented a survey team sent by the Canadian government from moving onto their lands. Led by Louis Riel, they seized Fort Garry, the colony's center. In a bold act, the Métis set up their own government for the colony. They barred the governor sent from Canada. Then they awaited negotiations with Ottawa.

The Métis government was opposed by many non-Métis in the colony. These people did not agree that rebellion would win better terms for the Métis or anyone else. Louis Riel was not popular with everyone. When his followers executed a Protestant English-speaking settler for attempting to overthrow his rule, the Canadian government in Ottawa chose to send troops rather than negotiate. Riel fled to the United States. The rebellion was over.

But the revolt had sown the seeds of division elsewhere in Canada. Riel and his followers were seen as treasonous rebels by Canada's English-speaking Protestant majority. In French-speaking Catholic Quebec, the view was different. Here he was seen as a patriot fighting in defense of his language and religion. These differences between the English and the French foreshadowed problems to come.

The Métis cause was not completely lost. In July, 1870, the small province of Manitoba was carved out of the Northwest Territories. The new province was established with guarantees for Métis land rights and the promise of language and religious freedom.

*The West needed law and order,
and the North-West Mounted Police provided it.*

**Law and order in the West.** With the rebellion crushed, the rest of the Northwest Territories now lay open. Much of it had not been explored and mapped.

How could such a large area be governed? Who would ensure orderly and peaceful development? Reports had already reached Ottawa that American whiskey traders were illegally crossing the border. It was said they cheated the Indians who lived there and encouraged drunkenness wherever they went. The whiskey traders even set up a trading post called Fort Whoop-Up on the Canadian side of the border, near the present-day city of Lethbridge, Alberta.

In 1873, the Canadian government acted. It wanted law and order in the west. It could not tolerate the lawless American wild west spilling over into Canada. The North-West Mounted Police (eventually renamed the Royal Canadian Mounted Police, or RCMP) was organized. A small troop of scarlet-coated officers was dispatched to maintain order. Though they were officially a police force, they soon won a reputation, especially among the native people, for peacefully upholding law and order. How different this was from the warlike tone that often marked relations between the Indians in the American West and the blue-coated U.S. army cavalry. In part because of the Mounties' even-handed administration of the law, and in part because that law was in force well before large-scale white settlement began, there were no significant Indian wars in the Canadian West. Eventually, the liquor trade was stamped out. Indian treaties were signed and the enormous Northwest Territories knew the rule of law.

**Canada reaches the Pacific.** Canada now stretched from the Atlantic to the Rocky Mountains. To the west of the mountains was the colony of British Columbia. As in the Red River Colony, there were those who wanted union with Canada. Others demanded union with the United States. Some preferred to remain a direct colony of Britain. Once again, promise of economic improvements and fear of U.S. designs led British Columbia to join Canada.

But Canada had to pay a price for British Columbia. First, it assumed the new province's debts. It also agreed to begin construction of a transcontinental railway. It would link British Columbia, through the rugged Rockies, across the vast prairies to eastern Canada. Ottawa promised to begin construction within two years and to finish the whole line within ten years.

**Building a transcontinental railway.** This was easier said than done. The construction of a railway to join all parts of Canada would be expensive. The federal government had neither the money nor the workers to do it. Efforts to encourage a private company to take on the task proved difficult. One scheme to do so ended in scandal. There were charges that the company's backers were not really Canadians but Americans. The Ottawa government was accused of paving the way for an American takeover. An election was called.

The new government did not put forward any suggestions on the railway issue. Only the return of Macdonald as prime minister after a few years time gave renewed initiative to the project. In 1880, a wealthy group of Canadian businessmen struck a deal to build the line. In return for their commitment, the government gave the new company, the Canadian Pacific, a number of advantages. It gave them all the track already completed, as well as vast tracts of land in the Canadian West for later resale. It gave them tax concessions and a big cash grant. The government promised that no competing railway would be built south of the proposed line. This gave the Canadian Pacific a transportation monopoly in what would eventually be the country's richest and most heavily populated farmlands.

The building of the Canadian Pacific Railway was one of the greatest business ventures in Canadian history. Cutting a railway line through the Rockies and across the Canadian Shield north of Lake Superior also proved to be among the great engineering efforts of all time. It rivaled the digging of the Panama Canal. An army of men, some working eastward from the Pacific, others pressing westward from Ontario, did not finish their job until 1885.

Some Canadians doubted the wisdom of the Canadian Pacific Railway. Before the work on it began, they warned that it would cost too much. As costs mounted, they seemed to be proved right. Where, they asked, was the advantage to Canadians or to the government in undertaking such a railway? In 1884, the answer came from an unexpected source. That year the still unfinished railway proved its worth to Ottawa. Unfortunately, its value was in carrying troops and supplies westward during the second Riel rebellion.

*Building the railway through the mountains was an incredible task!*

**The Riel Rebellion.** Problems with the Métis were stirring again. As track was laid across the prairies, surveyors once more moved onto Métis lands. This time it was not in the Red River Colony. It was farther west, in the southern Saskatchewan River valley. Some of these Métis had left the Red River Colony after the failure of their rebellion. As before, they had no guarantees for their land claims. They and many of the nearby Indians feared the railway would bring an influx of new settlers. The Indians had seen the disappearance of the buffalo herds on which they had depended for food and clothing. As a result, sickness and poverty had spread. Ottawa showed little concern with either Métis or Indian pleas. Again, the Métis wanted to negotiate. Again, Ottawa ignored them.

In 1884, they turned once more to Riel, who had been teaching school in Montana. He returned to lead them. At first he tried to strike a deal with Ottawa on the land issue. The government, however, was in no mood to compromise. Riel was still seen by many as a murderer. Rather than negotiate, the government responded with force. First came the Mounted Police. After shooting started and blood had been spilled, the army was sent in.

*Louis Riel was tried and sentenced in Regina, Saskatchewan.*

The new railroad already reached the western praries. So did the telegraph. Troops, munitions, and supplies were quickly dispatched westward. The rebellion was put down. Riel was captured, tried for treason, and eventually hanged.

Even as he awaited the hangman, Riel generated controversy. The English-French split that had marked the reaction to the first Métis rebellion surfaced again. To English Canadians, Riel was a traitor who deserved to be hung. To French Canadians, he was a martyr for his language, religion, and struggling fellow Métis. When he was hung, bitter feelings persisted between the two major language groups in Canada.

**Land without people.** With the completion of the railway, Canada was linked by rail from Atlantic to Pacific. A vast interior, the Northwest, lay open to settlement. Except for Newfoundland, which did not join Canada until 1949, the Canadian confederation "from sea to sea" had been forged. Canada's motto had become a reality.

But settlement of western Canada came slowly. Even when the railroad was completed in 1885, development did not materialize immediately. Few settlers from eastern Canada dashed off to settle the empty prairies.

Before the railway was available, most people heading for the Canadian Northwest made the long journey by way of the United States. They by-passed the difficult trek across the north shore of Lake Superior by traveling south of the Great Lakes through the American West. Many never re-entered Canada. While Ontario and Quebec were enormous in size, good farmland was scarce and heavily populated. Canadian manufacturing and urban employment were not large enough to absorb all those without land who were seeking jobs. As a result, thousands of Canadians crossed the border to seek their fortune in the United States. They were one of the largest immigrant groups entering the United States before the turn of the century.

From Quebec, many French Canadians made their way to the industrial towns and cities of nearby New England. French-Canadian sections sprang up in many American towns. French was spoken in many working-class neighborhoods. The French-Canadian Catholic church sent out priests to minister to the needs of their transplanted flock. They attempted to keep the French-Canadian way of life strong in the United States.

Many English Canadians from Ontario also ended up in the United States. Unlike the French, they did not seek out factory jobs. Instead, they joined the thousands of people filling up the farmlands of the American West. By the turn of the century, sons and daughters of Canadian farmers were scattered throughout the American Midwest and the prairie states.

This exodus reflected a Canadian problem. In spite of Confederation and the expansion "from sea to sea," Canada's economic growth was still painfully slow. What would the future hold? As the nineteenth century drew to a close, Canadians hoped the next one would be better.

# Double-check

**Review**

1. Name the British bill that officially created Canada.

2. In what two important ways was Canada still linked to Britain?

3. Who was Canada's first prime minister?

4. Who were the Métis?

5. In what year did Manitoba become the fifth province of Canada?

**Discussion**

1. During the first years after Confederation, English-speaking Canadians saw themselves as defenders of the British way of life in North America. Why do you think they felt so strongly about it? Do you think that attitude still persists today? Explain your answer.

2. Louis Riel was perhaps the most colorful and controversial figure in Canadian history. Discuss whether he was an inspired hero or a treasonous rebel. Do you think the Canadian government made a mistake in hanging him? Explain your answer.

3. Just before the turn of the century, a large number of Canadians went to live in the United States. Discuss the reasons for Canadian immigration to the United States at that time. Do you think some of those reasons still exist today? Explain.

**Activities**

1. Some students might want to read *Macdonald of Kingston*, or another biography about Sir John A. Macdonald, and describe to the class the qualities that made him a good man to lead Canada during the first years after Confederation.

2. Pretending to be Métis settlers in the Red River Colony, some students might write letters to the Canadian government in Ottawa stating specific grievances, suggesting solutions, and warning the government to act quickly.

3. Students might want to find out more about the "Mounties," the Royal Canadian Mounted Police — how they developed, what they do today, how their responsibilities have changed. "The Canadian Mounties — Past and Present" might be a good report title.

# *Skills*

## THE BRITISH NORTH AMERICA ACT

## BY THE QUEEN.
# A PROCLAMATION
## For Uniting the Provinces of Canada, Nova Scotia, and New Brunswick into One Dominion under the Name of CANADA.

VICTORIA R.

WHEREAS by an Act of Parliament passed on the Twenty-ninth Day of March One thousand eight hundred and sixty-seven, in the Thirtieth Year of Our Reign, intituled " An Act for the Union of Canada, Nova Scotia, and New Brunswick, and the " Government thereof, and for Purposes connected therewith," after divers Recitals, it is enacted, that " it shall be lawful for the Queen, by and with the Advice of Her Majesty's most Honorable " Privy Council, to declare by Proclamation that on and after a Day therein appointed, not being " more than Six Months after the passing of this Act, the Provinces of Canada, Nova Scotia, and " New Brunswick shall form and be One Dominion under the Name of Canada, and on and after " that Day those Three Provinces shall form and be One Dominion under that Name accordingly:" And it is thereby further enacted, that " such Persons shall be first summoned to the Senate as " the Queen, by Warrant under Her Majesty's Royal Sign Manual, thinks fit to approve, and " their Names shall be inserted in the Queen's Proclamation of Union:" We therefore, by and with the Advice of Our Privy Council, have thought fit to issue this Our Royal Proclamation, and We do Ordain, Declare, and Command, that on and after the First Day of July One thousand eight hundred and sixty-seven the Provinces of Canada, Nova Scotia, and New Brunswick shall form and be One Dominion under the Name of Canada. And We do further Ordain and Declare, that the Persons whose Names are herein inserted and set forth are the Persons of whom We have, by Warrant under Our Royal Sign Manual, thought fit to approve as the Persons who shall be first summoned to the Senate of Canada.

Given at Our Court at Windsor Castle, this Twenty-second Day of May, in the Year of our Lord One thousand eight hundred and sixty-seven, and in the Thirtieth Year of Our Reign.

## God save the Queen.

Source: Public Archives

*Use the replica above and information in Chapter 9 to answer the following questions.*

1. What was the purpose of this proclamation?

2. What was the date of the proclamation?

3. Where was the proclamation given?

4. Most of the people "first summoned to the Senate of Canada" were from Ontario and Quebec. Why was that so?

5. Canada has a Latin motto: *A Mari Usque ad Mare*. What does this mean in English?

# Chapter 10

# Dawning of the Twentieth Century

Before the turn of the century, the Canadian West remained largely empty. The Indian and Métis land claims had already been resolved. The Canadian Pacific Railway was complete. Police patrolled the land. It only awaited settlers, and they were not long in coming.

**The last best West.** Several factors combined to make settlement of western Canada more attractive by the turn of the century. After years of declining markets, the international market for wheat had begun to develop. The Canadian prairies promised to be among the best wheat growing regions in the world. There was, however, one major problem. On the Canadian prairies, the growing season was shorter. Spring arrived later than on the U.S. prairies and winter came earlier. Wheat needed more time to grow, and early frost frequently destroyed the crop. A new variety of wheat was needed, one that could grow and ripen in a much shorter time. A new strain, called Marquis wheat, was developed. It was of exceptional quality and it matured within a very short growing period. This made the prospect of wheat farming in Western Canada very attractive and encouraged new settlers.

Thousands of settlers from many parts of the world began streaming into the Canadian West. Western Canada was booming, and the government and railway were determined the boom should not stop. The government wanted agricultural settlers and the Canadian Pacific Railway wanted customers. They jointly offered special deals.

The railway encouraged immigrants with low steamship and railway fares, while the government offered free land grants. The immigrants who came to western Canada hoped Prime Minister Wilfred Laurier was right when he said, "The twentieth century belongs to Canada."

Many of those Canadians and non-Canadians who now flocked into the Canadian West would have gone to the American West. However, by the early 1900's good farmland in the western United States was increasingly scarce. The era of the U.S. agricultural frontier was over. Almost a million U.S. farmers now crossed the border to take up land in Canada. They settled in what they called the "last best West."

*A Ruthenian home in St. Paul de Métis, Alberta.*

Farming was not the only area of economic growth. During railway construction through the Canadian Shield and the Rockies, previously unknown or hard-to-reach Canadian resources were opened for development. Major stands of timber were now available for logging. In addition, silver, nickel, copper, and iron were soon being mined for export.

In 1896, a prospector working his way across the Yukon made a discovery. He found a rich vein of gold and staked his claim. As the news of the find leaked out, gold fever spread. The famous Klondike Gold Rush was on. Before long, thousands of gold-hungry adventurers from all over the world began trekking overland across the snow-covered coastal mountains into the Yukon. All were fired with dreams of instant wealth. Only a few would realize those dreams. Most were disappointed and left empty-handed after a few years.

**The Alaska boundary dispute.** The gold rush soon raised a thorny diplomatic problem. Many of those who made their way into the Yukon came first by boat to the small ports in the Pacific Northwest. Ownership of this land was in dispute between the United States and Canada. When the United States bought Alaska from Russia in 1867, the border between the Alaskan panhandle and British Columbia had not been fixed. An exact border was not a high priority at the time, since there were so few people in the region. Suddenly the situation changed as more people arrived for the gold rush. An exact border became necessary.

The Americans demanded the border be drawn far enough inland to give them control of the numerous coastal inlets. Canada also wanted a northern Pacific port to service northern British Columbia and the Yukon. Canada pressed for a border agreement that would give it access to the mouth of one or more deepwater inlets where a Canadian port could be constructed.

# ALASKA BOUNDARY DISPUTE 1903

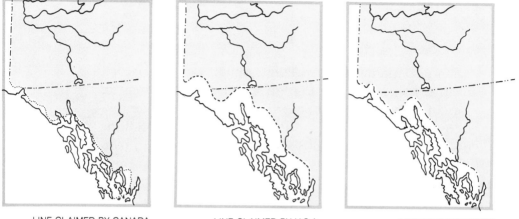

LINE CLAIMED BY CANADA — LINE CLAIMED BY U.S.A. — LINE OF SETTLEMENT

To settle the dispute, the British, who still handled Canadian international relations, suggested that an impartial panel decide the case. A panel of six persons was set up in 1903, with three American, two Canadian and one British representative.

The panel proved a bitter disappointment to Canada. American President Teddy Roosevelt chose three outspoken backers of the American position rather than three impartial representatives. The British representative also voted with the Americans. At the time, Britain needed American cooperation on a whole range of international problems. To the British, Canada's desire for access to the north Pacific was less important than ensuring continued American friendship. As a result, Canada lost that access.

Canadians were furious at being "sold out." They felt cheated by the Americans and betrayed by the British. Many Canadians began to feel that Canada, a self-governing country within the Empire, should manage its own international affairs without British interference.

**Canadian participation in the Boer War.** The Boers were descendants of the early Dutch settlers in South Africa. In 1899, they declared their territories independent from Britain, which ruled South Africa as a colony. Britain dispatched troops against the Boers to put down their rebellion.

Many Canadians, especially English Canadians, felt that any threat to the British Empire was a threat to Canada. Canada, they argued, was a part of the Empire and had a duty to defend it. Many French Canadians disagreed. They saw no Boer threat to Canada. In fact, their sympathies were with the Boers, who seemed much like themselves — a small group struggling to retain their language, religion, and way of life.

In 1902, the year before the Alaska boundary discussion, the British officially requested Canadian troops to assist in the Boer War. The Canadian government was torn between the conflicting views of French and English Canadians. In the end, it compromised. Almost 8,000 Canadian troops were dispatched to fight in South Africa, but all were volunteers. No Canadian soliders who disagreed with the war were forced to go. Those who went made an important contribution to the eventual British victory. For English Canadians, the triumph of British arms was not just a triumph for Britain, but one for the British Empire in which Canada was a partner.

Pride in victory against the Boers and disappointment at the "betrayal" in Alaska fed Canadian patriotism. Many Canadians came to believe that *full* Canadian independence within the Empire was not only possible but necessary.

**Defense of the Empire.** Events in Europe gave this argument new meaning. In the first decade of the century, Germany and Britain began a naval arms race. The British called on the Empire for assistance. They wanted all the self-governing countries of the Empire, like Australia, New Zealand, and Canada, to fund the construction of ships for the British navy. Canada refused. It was not prepared to pay for warships that would not be commanded by Canadians.

Canadians knew they would rush to the defense of Britain in the event of war with Germany. But they wanted to do it in Canada's name. Rather than build ships for the British navy, the government set aside money to build its own warships for a new Royal Canadian Navy. With this action, the country took yet another step toward determining its own destiny.

The Canadian navy and, indeed, all Canadians were soon put to the test. In Europe, events looked bleak. Germany and Britain had pulled their allies together in a series of mutual-defense alliances. The treaties were set up so that if any ally of Germany went to war with any ally of Britain, eventually Britain and Germany would be swept into the conflict. It was like a house of cards. If one card fell, the whole structure would collapse.

In June, 1914, the first card fell. An assassination in southeastern Europe set off a chain reaction. As allies of Britain and Germany began fighting with one another, it was only a matter of time before the two countries were drawn into the battle. War did not explode. Peace fell apart. In early August, Britain declared war on Germany. Canada also considered itself at war. The First World War had begun.

Though Canadians rallied to the aid of Britain, the country was unprepared for war. Canada had only 3,000 men in uniform, a tiny navy and no airforce. But in the first flush of enthusiasm for "the war to end all wars," many lined up to volunteer. There was no draft. Those who volunteered recalled the short and glorious Boer War. They thought of the might of the British fleet. How could this war be anything less than a swift crusade leading to British victory? It was a war not to be missed. In a few months and with minimal training, almost 35,000 Canadian troops were shipped to Britain. In 1915, two years before the United States entered the war, Canadians were dug into the trenches of France and Belgium. Across a narrow no man's land, the Germans were also dug in.

*Canadian pilot Billy Bishop brought down a total of 72 enemy planes.*

*Preparing for a gas attack.*

Whatever notions the Canadians had of a short and glorious war were lost in the mud and death in France and Belgium. During four years of cruel battle, they endured the worst the Germans could offer. They returned it in kind. Death, disease, pain, and fear were the lot of all those who served in the front lines. The Canadians fought well and repeatedly distinguished themselves for bravery. Canadian troops dug in at Ypres in Belgium were among the first to suffer the horror of deadly German gas attacks.

They also volunteered in large numbers for the Royal Air Force. At the height of the war, one-third of all Royal Air Force pilots were Canadians.

By the time the war ended in November, 1918, 60,000 Canadians had given their lives "for king and country." That was the last time a British declaration of war was binding on Canada.

**The homefront.** The homefront was not without its problems. Universal support for the war effort evaporated as the war dragged on. In Quebec, many came to see the war not as a battle for Canada but as a battle to save Britain. For many French Canadians, this was a foreign cause. Voluntary recruitment for the military, especially within Quebec, began to decline. As casualties mounted in Europe, the military demanded more men. The government had little choice. It decided on conscription to draft men into uniform. Quebec remained hostile to conscription. Bitterness grew. Violence between French-speaking and English-speaking Canadians threatened. Luckily, the war ended before the government was forced to take severe measures against draft dodgers.

The war also brought great economic and social changes. As demands for military and other supplies grew, Canadian industry expanded to meet those demands. Canada had long struggled to develop its own

*Many women became factory workers during the war. This group operated cartridge case presses.*

manufacturing capacity to compete with British and American imports. Now it had its chance. During the war, emergency industrial output mushroomed. Factories were producing items Canadians had never dreamed of manufacturing on a large scale — airplanes, guns and munitions, trucks and cars. By the end of the war, the country was on the verge of becoming an industrial power.

With so many men in uniform, women were encouraged to move from the kitchen to the factory. Partly in response to the women's war effort, Canadian women were granted the vote. In 1917, the vote was given to women in uniform and to wives and mothers of those in uniform. The following year it was extended to all Canadian women. This was several years before women in the United States won the vote.

When the war ended in 1918, thousands of men came back from the trenches of Europe. They found a changed Canada. For many, it was not necessarily a better Canada. To be sure, new industries had taken root. Many Canadians had contributed fully to the national war effort. There was much pride in achievement. But there were also problems. Those who had given so much expected to return from the war to waiting jobs and property. Many would be disappointed. Once the war ended, the demand for war materials disappeared. Manufacturing slowed to a crawl. Workers were let go. Jobs were hard to find. Many discharged soldiers moved from the front lines to the unemployment lines. Strikes and industrial unrest broke out everywhere.

During the "roaring twenties," Canadians, like Americans, went on a buying spree. Half of all families owned a car. Everyone seemed to own a radio. Electrically powered appliances — stoves, refrigerators, radios — were made attractive by the availability of cheap electricity.

Electricity was generated from newly tapped sources of water power such as Niagara Falls. This power source also served the needs of the expanding mining and pulp and paper industries. As Canadian and foreign manufacturing increased, so did the demand for Canadian raw materials.

Not all the business enterprise was strictly legal. Most provinces prohibited the sale of liquor during the war. In postwar times, the anti-liquor crusade died out. Liquor sales were allowed again in most of Canada. In the United States, however, liquor prohibition was built into the Constitution. It was against the law in the United States to import or sell alcohol. But illegal or not, Americans wanted liquor. And there were those in Canada only too ready to supply it for a profit.

Liquor smuggling into the United States grew. Rum-running boats and trucks crossed the border at isolated points in the dead of night. American border guards tried to stamp out the smuggling, but it was an almost impossible task. Canadian officials usually refused to help. Since there was no prohibition in Canada, no Canadian laws were being broken.

**The Great Depression.** In Canada, as in the United States, the prosperity of the 1920's was built on very thin ice. Too many individuals and companies had bought goods or expanded their operations on borrowed money. When demand for Canadian raw materials and manufactured goods slowed down, many people and businesses did not have the money on hand to pay their debts. Banks and other creditors demanded their money. Businesses by the score could not pay and went bankrupt. Tens of thousands of people were soon unemployed. The prosperous 20's gave way to the Great Depression of the 30's.

The Depression was made worse by a severe drought in the West. Rich prairie farmland became parched desert. Farmers were unable to produce food, and therefore could not pay mortgages. Countless farm families had to abandon their land and move to the cities in search of jobs. There they competed with unemployed industrial workers. Jobs were rare. "No Help Wanted" signs were everywhere. More than one-third of all Canadians were out of work.

In desperation, thousands turned to welfare. But the Canadian welfare system was poor. Unlike today, there was no social security system, no unemployment bene-fits, no medicare program. City, provincial, and federal governments and private charities were soon strapped for funds. They did what they could, but it was never enough. Hunger was common. In winter, many fami-lies did not have enough fuel or clothing to keep warm. Misery was the lot of millions.

**The Winnipeg General Strike.** In Winnipeg, Mani-toba, industrial unrest in 1919 exploded into a general strike of almost all workers in the city. This was a landmark in Canadian labor history. The strike began with those in the building and metal trades. After two weeks on the picket line, they were joined by sym-pathetic workers in most other areas. Business in

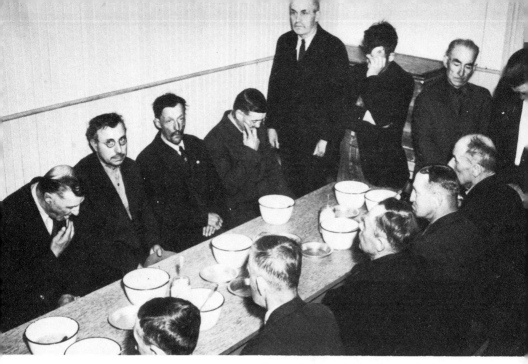

*Depression was both a fact and a feeling.*

*Angry crowds brought Winnipeg to a standstill in 1919.*

Winnipeg ground to a halt. Government service, transportation, and communication workers walked out. A central strike committee, however, made sure essential services were kept going. Police, for instance, were asked by the strike committee to stay on the job even though they had also voted to strike. Workers demanded higher wages and official recognition for newly organized unions.

Business and industrial leaders in Winnipeg were upset and angry. They did not want to give in to the workers' demands. Instead, they accused the strike leaders of being dangerous foreign agents of communism. It was only two years since the 1917 Russian Revolution. Many feared the "red menace" could spread to North America. Was the Winnipeg strike a local matter, or would it spread across Canada and into the United States? If it was not crushed in Winnipeg, employers warned, there would be no end to it.

As employers refused to negotiate, peaceful demonstrations and workers' marches grew ugly. The government moved in on the side of business leaders. Soon violence broke out. Strike leaders were arrested and riots followed. Before order could be restored, troops had to be brought in. The strike collapsed. Bitterness remained. The struggle to organize strong labor unions was set back, but the goal was not forgotten.

With the end of the Winnipeg General Strike, a hectic postwar era drew to a close. Canadians might not have realized it then, but their world had changed dramatically in only one generation. From the turn of the century through the era of mass western settlement, the First World War, and its aftermath, Canada was a transformed land. It had changed from a small, rural country to a major resource exporter and industrial country. It was no longer attached to its colonial past. It was proud of its achievements and watchful of its independence.

# Double-check

## Review

1. How did the Canadian government and the Canadian Pacific Railway encourage settlers to the West?

2. What event brought many new people to the Yukon?

3. How many Canadians were killed in battle during World War I?

4. In what year was the vote first given to Canadian women?

5. How did Canada change between the turn of the century and the end of World War I?

## Discussion

1. Why did Canadians feel betrayed by the British in the Alaska boundary dispute? Do you think their feelings were justified? Why or why not?

2. Why were many French Canadians not interested in participating in the Boer War or in World War I? Discuss their attitude. Explain why you agree or disagree with their point of view.

3. The Winnipeg General Strike marked the beginning of Canadian labor history. Why are unions important in a democratic society? What are the pros and cons of having strikes? Who benefits and who loses?

## Activities

1. Students might write a diary entry of a prospector in the Yukon during the Klondike Gold Rush. They might detail his discoveries (or disappointments), and his plans for the future.

2. Some students might want to find out more about the war effort of Canadian women during World War I, and how it led to their right to vote. They might look for information about such women as Nellie McLung, Frances Beynon, Dr. Stowe-Gullen, or Carrie Derick, and give an oral report on one of them.

3. Some might find out about Canadians on the European front, especially in such places as Ypres or Vimy Ridge. A group of students might playact recently returned war veterans being interviewed by reporters at a press conference. War experiences and problems in adjusting after returning home might be discussed.

# Skills

## CANADA'S GOVERNMENT

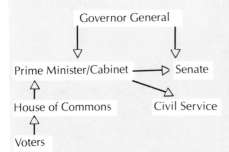

In Canada, the voters from each province and territory elect representatives to the *House of Commons*, the law-making body of the country. These representatives usually belong to political parties. The leader of the party with the greatest number of seats (representatives) becomes the head of government, the *Prime Minister*. The *Cabinet*, made up of leading members of the party in power, is chosen by the Prime Minister to help lead the government. They plan, execute, and enforce the laws passed by the House of Commons, with the help of *Civil Servants*, who are employees of the government. The *Governor General* represents the monarch in Canada and gives official "royal assent" to all laws. The *Senate* is a group of appointed advisors who review proposals before they become laws.

The federal government of Canada, described above, is in charge of matters that concern the country as a whole: for example, trade, citizenship, the postal service. Each province also has its own government in charge of matters such as education and hospitals.

*Use the information above to answer the following questions.*

1. The real power in the Canadian government is in the House of Commons. Where do its members come from?

2. Members of the Canadian Cabinet are often called Ministers. How do Ministers get into the Cabinet?

3. What does the word *prime* mean? Why is the head of the Canadian government called the Prime Minister?

4. What is the Governor General's connection with Britain?

5. What is the meaning of the term *federal government* in Canada? What is the meaning of the term *provincial government*?

# Chapter 11

# The Modern Era

The postwar economic slowdown gradually eased. Export markets for Canadian raw materials and manufactured goods picked up. Assembly lines were humming. Mines were reopened. The railroads were busy carrying resources and industrial products to ports crowded with ships. For many Canadians, the most important fact of prosperity was that jobs were easier to find.

Prosperity and growth seemed to be everywhere. Factories opened. Cities expanded. More and more Canadians were now choosing city life and wage labor rather than farming. By 1930, half of all Canadians lived in cities.

At first, Canadians had faith in recovery. Business, they hoped, would bounce back. If not, the government would cope with what many were sure was but a temporary economic setback. They were wrong. It was not temporary. The Depression dragged on for a decade. The governments in power seemed as short of ideas for dealing with the Depression as citizens were short of money to buy basic needs.

**The New Politics.** Canada found no political leader like American President Franklin Delano Roosevelt to inspire hope. There was no New Deal to cushion the crisis. In Ottawa, there seemed not enough political will, imagination, or, most important, money to wrestle with the Depression. Perhaps there was little any Canadian political leadership could have done. So long as the Depression was worldwide, there were no markets available.

Some Canadians looked beyond the two traditional Canadian political parties — the Liberals and the Conservatives — for a political solution. These two older parties could trace their roots back to the era before Canadian Confederation. Like Democrats and Republicans in the United States, one or the other had always held federal and provincial political power.

But it seemed to some Canadians that neither of the old parties was able to cope with the crisis. In the Canadian West, where the Depression hit the hardest, new radical political parties won many supporters. The most important of these was the Canadian Commonwealth Federation (C.C.F.). The C.C.F. was a democratic socialist party. Its followers argued for public welfare service to protect all Canadians and a government takeover of basic industries. They believed the development of a national policy for economic growth was the best road to recovery. Unlike the small Canadian Communist Party, the C.C.F. was dedicated to the Canadian democratic system.

The C.C.F. never attracted a large enough following to achieve national power. But many of its ideas were eventually adopted by the two traditional parties. Unlike Americans, Canadians were ready, if necessary for the public good, to have their governments own and operate business enterprises. Few private companies could or would provide necessary services without guarantee of profit. With so small a population and so vast a

Prominent C.C.F. leaders: J.S. Woodsworth (left)
and T.C. Douglas (right). Both men were preachers.

territory, profit was not always possible. But certain services were essential. As a result, governments in Canada have felt obligated to enter into business, sometimes in competition with private industry.

In 1921, during the tail end of the postwar slump, a group of railroads in competition with the powerful Canadian Pacific fell on hard times. They had over-expanded during the war and now were losing money. The government realized that Canadians could not do without the service and took over the failing railroads. It tied them together to form a second transcontinental railroad, the Canadian National. To this day, the Canadian National remains government owned and operated.

Again borrowing from the C.C.F. program, the federal government organized a national radio network, the Canadian Broadcasting Corporation (CBC) and a national airline, Trans-Canada Airlines, now renamed Air Canada. Both these public services are still owned and operated by the federal government. Other federally and provincially owned businesses, including electric and other public utilities, were also established during this era.

**World War II.** The Depression finally ended. It was not, however, successful government programs or a recovery of private business that brought back prosperity. It was war.

In Germany, the Depression and unstable government eventually brought the Nazis to power. The Nazi dictator, Adolph Hitler, had two goals. He wanted to expand German power in Europe. And he wanted to prove the "racial superiority" of the German people, even if it meant mass murder of other people. All efforts to appease Hitler's ambition to dominate Europe failed. In September, 1939, Germany invaded Poland. Britain declared war.

This time Canada did not feel itself automatically and officially at war because Britain was. Several years earlier, in 1931, the British parliament had passed the Statute of Westminster, at Canada's request. This legislation declared that no act of the British parliament was binding on Canada. Canada was truly an independent country within the British Empire, which had now been transformed into the British Commonwealth.

There was no doubt, however, that Canada would join the war against Hitler. Several days after Britain declared war, the Canadian parliament met. It, too, declared war on Germany. As in World War I, this was more than two years before the United States officially entered the war.

Once more, Canada was unprepared for battle. When war broke out, only 10,000 Canadians were in uniform. Between September, 1939, and August, 1945, when the war ended in Allied victory, more than a million Canadians, almost 10 percent of the total population, served in the armed forces. Canadians would mourn more than 41,000 killed in battle.

Canadian troops again served with distinction. The Royal Canadian Air Force, organized after World War I, joined the Battle of Britain. Together with other fliers, they inflicted heavy losses on the German bombers that attacked British cities night after night in 1940. German losses were eventually so great that Hitler was forced to call off the mass bombings. His plans for an invasion of Britain were destroyed.

Thousands of Allied fliers were sent to Canada for training. When air attacks against German cities began, Canadian bombers and crews flew side by side with the Allies.

On the high seas, the Royal Canadian Navy concentrated its efforts in the North Atlantic. The navy took responsibility for much convoy escort duty. It was their job to ensure that supplies from the United States and Canada crossed the Atlantic safely. Canadian seamen were crucial in breaking the back of German submarine warfare in the North Atlantic.

*Canadians entered Cannes, France, a few days after D-Day, June 6, 1944.*

On the ground, Canadian servicemen fought in the defense of Hong Kong against the more powerful Japanese invading army. Canadian troops also battled the Germans in Italy and were part of the 1944 Normandy invasion that finally crushed Nazi power in Europe. They went on to assist in the liberation of France, Belgium, and Holland. In the spring of 1945, Canadians accepted the surrender of the German army facing them in Holland.

**An industrial nation.** The country's contribution to the war effort went beyond the sacrifice of men and women in uniform. Canada, second only to the United States, was the major supplier of war materials and financial loans to the Allies. Canadian industry again converted to production of aircraft, warships, and weapons. Food, clothing, medical supplies, and almost everything else needed for the war effort were dispatched. Canadian scientists worked on war-related intelligence and research tasks. Canadians were part of the team that developed the atomic bomb.

As in World War I, the war against Hitler ushered in changes in the status of women. Labor shortages put many women into uniform or overalls. Women were crucial in every area of the economy.

Industrial output grew and farm production steadily increased. Canada shipped much of its production abroad. At home, rationing was imposed. Gasoline, butter, and sugar, among other things, remained in short supply. Taxes were raised to cover the costs of the war. Everyone was encouraged to lend the government money by buying war bonds.

Not all was harmonious on the home front, however. World War II again heightened tension between English-speaking and French-speaking Canadians. Although many French Canadians enlisted and fought overseas, French Canada was still against conscription. The federal government hoped to avoid a second crisis over conscription by sending only volunteers overseas. When the draft was first imposed, it was designed for a home-guard, not for overseas duty.

Finally war needs in Europe proved greater than the supply of Canadian volunteers could successfully fill. It was decided that draftees should be sent to Europe. French Canada and many of those who had been drafted for the homeguard were angry. Some protested and even threatened not to go. Luckily, the war ended before this second conscription crisis could cause more damage to national unity.

**The postwar period.** When the war ended in the summer of 1945, many Canadians feared that the Great Depression of the 1930's would return. With no further need for Canadian war materials, what would keep factories busy? Where would battle-hardened veterans find employment?

The Depression did not return. The reverse occurred. Many people had saved or invested money earned during the war. After the war, they were prepared to spend. They wanted consumer goods that had been rationed or unavailable during the Depression and the war. In addition, there was need to rebuild war-shattered Europe. This created an almost unending demand for Canadian raw materials, manufactured goods, and food products. Canada now moved from the full employment of war to the full employment of postwar. Rather than unemployment, there were continuing labor shortages.

A stronger economy was not the only difference between the prewar and postwar eras. After the trials of the Great Depression and the sacrifices of the war, Canada seemed a country reawakened and reshaped. Its economy was not just stronger. It was also more technologically up-to-date and competitive. With an

*Up-to-date technology brought important advances. The main dam at this generating station is 2400 feet (732 meters) long and 180 feet (55 meters) high.*

increased demand for Canadian goods on the world market, factories expanded. Cities began to grow again. As farms became mechanized, more people moved off the land. Canada became one of the most urban countries in the world.

**Canada and the world.** Prosperity and the self-assured role Canada played during the war brought increased recognition on the international stage. Canada helped to organize the United Nations and played a key role in solving many of the international problems of the postwar era. It became a founding member of the North Atlantic Treaty Organization (NATO). When the Korean War broke out in 1950, Canadian troops were among those that came to the defense of South Korea. Canadian troops continue to serve with the United Nations peace teams in various hot spots around the globe.

*Peace-keeping on the Egypt-Israel frontier.*

Canada also played a new role within the British Commonwealth. The Empire, with Britain at its head, was now a thing of the past. Colonies in Africa, Asia, and the Caribbean pressed forward to full independence. Canada was often their model. Like Canada, these new independent countries chose to maintain membership in the Commonwealth. Today, they represent many different political ideologies, languages, and races. In spite of their differences, they voluntarily continue to assist one another and discuss issues of mutual concern. The Commonwealth is now a forum for the exchange of views and aid.

What of the old British connection? Is it more than a historical memory for Canadians? While the British monarch is still the queen of Canada, the country has asserted its full independence from Britain. No act of the British parliament is valid in Canada. In the past, citizens of Britain who wished to immigrate to Canada could enter at will. Today they must apply for immigration the same as anyone else in the world.

Oddly, the coming of full maturity has caused some difficulties for Canadian national identity, especially English-speaking Canada. Before World War II, many English Canadians felt comfortable with the notion that being a Canadian meant being a British subject in North America. Canadians took pride in their country, but did so by preserving links to British traditions. Being part of the British Empire was an important symbol of that British tradition.

After the war, the Empire faded from its previous glory. Canada asserted independence of action and mind. The British connection was far less significant. As a result, there was a need to re-evaluate the foundation of the national identity. Canadians, especially English-speaking Canadians, had to build a new identity as a free people in North America.

Immigration has been one of the key forces in bringing about a new Canadian identity. Since the first settlers arrived in North America centuries ago, millions of people from all over the world have made Canada home. In recent years, this immigration has helped redefine the notion of who is a Canadian. Just as we have explored the country's geography and history, it is now important to explore the growth of the Canadian people.

# Double-check

## Review

1. In which decade did the Great Depression occur?

2. What two strategies did the new C.C.F. party promote?

3. How many Canadians served in the armed forces during World War II?

4. What contributions did Canadian industry make to the war?

5. Canada joined two international organizations formed after the war. What were they?

## Discussion

1. By 1930, half of all Canadians lived in cities. Discuss the reasons for this. Is it good for a country to have so much of its population in urban centers? Why or why not?

2. The C.C.F. and its successor, the NDP (New Democratic Party), have never been in power, but their ideas have often been adopted by the other parties. Why? How do you think the NDP, with its interest in the working class and organized labor, has contributed to Canada? How does its existence as an influential party make Canada a different country from the United States?

3. The Statute of Westminster, which transformed the British Empire into the British Commonwealth, declared that no future act of British Parliament would be binding on Canada. Discuss the events that led to this pronouncement.

## Activities

1. Students might research Canadian participation in one of the battles during World War II: Dunkirk, Dieppe, Ortona, or Normandy. They might pretend to be Canadian soldiers describing their experiences in letters home.

2. Two groups might each research and report on one of the major political parties in Canada, the Liberals and the Conservatives: their history, their past and current leaders, their policies, their similarities (if any) to the Democratic and Republican parties in the United States.

3. Some might find out more about Canada's involvement in the United Nations and NATO, then debate the following question and take a vote: Do you think participation in the UN and NATO is good for Canada?

# Skills

## A CITATION FOR BRAVERY: WORLD WAR II

More than 41,000 Canadians died serving in World War II. A number were awarded the Victoria Cross for bravery. Here is the story of one of these courageous people.

Pilot Officer Andrew Charles Mynarski
BORN: Winnipeg, October 14, 1916
SERVICE: Royal Canadian Air Force
DIED: Near Cambrai, France, June 12, 1944
V.C.: Awarded Posthumously

Pilot Officer Mynarski was the mid-upper gunner of a Lancaster aircraft detailed to attack a target at Cambrai in France, on the night of 12th June, 1944. The aircraft was attacked from below and astern by an enemy fighter ...Fire broke out...and the captain ordered the crew to abandon the air-craft...Mynarski left his turret and went towards the escape hatch. He then saw that the rear gunner was still in his turret and apparently unable to leave it...

Without hesitation...Mynarski made his way through the flames in an endeavor to reach the rear turret and release the gunner. Whilst so doing, his parachute and his clothing, up to the waist, were set on fire. All his efforts to move the turret and free the gunner were in vain. Eventually the rear gunner clearly indicated to him that there was nothing more he could do and that he should try to save his own life. Pilot Officer Mynarski reluctantly went back through the flames to the escape hatch. There, as a last gesture to the trapped gunner, he turned towards him, stood to attention in his flaming clothes and saluted, before he jumped out of the aircraft...He was found eventually by the French, but was so severely burnt that he died from his injuries.
(The rear gunner miraculously survived the crash.)

Source: *Valiant Men: Canada's Victoria Cross and George Cross Winners*, edited by John Swettenham, Canadian War Museum Historical Publication, 1973.

*Use the story above and information in Chapter 11 to answer the following questions.*

1. The story above comes from what kind of source?
   (a) government statistics
   (b) collection of true stories about war heroes
   (c) war novel written by Andrew Charles Mynarski

2. What is the Victoria Cross awarded for?

3. In the story above, why did the captain order the crew to leave the aircraft?

4. Why did Pilot Officer Mynarski turn back after he started toward the escape hatch?

5. What do Mynarski's actions in the story tell you about the kind of person he was?

5

THE

PEOPLE

# Chapter 12

# The Founding Peoples

Perhaps nowhere has the Canadian struggle to develop
a unique Canadian identity in North America been
more evident than in the peopling of the country.
Canadians can trace their origins to every corner of the
globe. Except for the native people, all Canadians share
an immigrant heritage, whether from this generation
or an earlier one. Immigrants have arrived in Canada
with more than their hopes for the future. They also
carried cultural backpacks overflowing with a wealth of
traditions from their homelands.

Canadians have attempted to accommodate these
different cultures. It has not always been easy. Like
Americans, Canadians encourage a shared sense of
national pride. They are attempting to do this through
the preservation and development of many different
cultural traditions dwelling side by side in one land.

**The Canadian Mosaic.** Both Canada and the United States have accepted millions of settlers from every corner of the world. But there is a sharp difference. In the United States, the focus has been on encouraging a single American way of life. Canadians, however, have rejected the "melting pot" idea. They have developed a different notion of how immigrants should be absorbed. They are proud of the richness of the traditions and cultures that together make up what they call "the Canadian mosaic."

If you look closely at a mosaic, you will find many separate parts. Each is different in size, shape, and color from the others. Each piece is unique in itself but all pieces are held to a common surface by the same mortar. If you look at it from a distance, you know individual pieces are still there. But you don't really see them. Instead, you see the full picture, of which each piece is a valued part.

Canadian society has been described as a mosaic of many cultures, many traditions, and many different ways of life. Each element of the Canadian cultural mosaic is distinct. Each is precious. Together they form a unity made stronger and more interesting because of its many parts.

The concept of the mosaic did not develop overnight. Indeed, before World War II, many Canadians felt that there was little or nothing in the traditions and cultures of other peoples that was worth preserving or developing in Canada. Some were motivated by a well-meaning desire to assimilate both immigrants and native peoples. Others were expressing a deep-seated prejudice against anyone different from themselves. For whichever reason, most Canadians, especially in English-speaking Canada, did not think of Canada as an evolving mosaic of cultures. They wanted everyone to become model English Canadians, guardians of the British way of life in North America.

**The native people.** Native people joke that if their forefathers had enforced a more restrictive immigration policy there might not be any other Canadians to worry about. The native people, of course, could never have controlled the arrival of new people in North America as both the United States and Canada do today. But the arrival of the European settlers did dramatically reshape the life of the native people.

As we have already learned, Canada's native people are descendents of those migrant hunters who crossed from Asia to North America before modern history. Although today they constitute only a small fraction of Canada's population, less than four percent, the native people are Canada's original inhabitants. As such, they claim a special place within the Canadian family of peoples.

For many years, Canada's "First Nations" remained far from center stage in the public mind. Until recently, most Canadians fully expected that over time the native people would be absorbed into the Canadian mainstream and disappear as a distinct group. Public schooling in the past encouraged them toward this goal.

But they did not disappear. Most did not turn their backs on their culture and heritage. They did not choose to simply blend into the larger Canadian community. Nor are they any longer content to remain in the shadows. They have emerged to demand special status and justice for wrongs inflicted on them in the past.

It would be wrong, however, to think of these native people as a single group, unified from coast to coast. In spite of their shared sense of being Canada's original people and having suffered injustice at the hands of later arrivals, the native people of Canada are not united. They represent a patchwork of different groups. They are separated from one another by different languages, different tribal traditions, different religious

155

heritages, and different levels of interaction with non-native Canadians. They are also spread thinly across the Canadian landscape. Only in the far North do they constitute a sizable portion of the total population.

In addition, many have joined the larger Canadian drift into urban centers. Some have not found this an easy adjustment. Some have become part of the urban poor. Others, with pride in their past, have carved out lives for themselves in business or the professions.

In spite of their differences, they have all recently demonstrated a sharpened sense of shared pride in their native roots. They have an enormous stake in current discussions with the government on the special status of the native people in Canadian society. Basically they fall into four categories:

*Prominent native leaders.*

*Wallace Labillois, Micmac, N.B.*     *Chief Billy Diamond, Cree, Que.*     *Chief Gary Potts, Algonquin, Ont*

*Harold Cardinal, Cree, Alta.*     *Neil Sterritt, Gatksan, B.C.*

**The status Indians.** This group already has official recognition as native people in the eyes of the law. They are covered by the federal Indian Act. That act outlines the duties and the responsibilities of the federal government in caring for status Indians.

Many status Indians, especially those in the southern half of Canada, long ago negotiated land treaties with the government. In those treaties, they gave up the bulk of their lands and were relocated onto reserves. Today most status Indians still make their homes on those reserves. Unfortunately, poverty is a way of life on many of them. Others house a thriving industry or business, and prosper. Some receive royalties for natural resources, such as oil or timber, found on their lands.

Dr. David Ahenakew, CM, CD, Cree, Sask.

Chief Sol Sanderson, Cree, Sask.

Chief Rod Robinson, Nishga, B.C.    Chief Tom Sampson, Coast Salish, B.C.    Georges Erasmus, Denendeh, N.W.T.

The special talents of community members may also mean prosperity. The Mohawks on the Caughnawaga Reserve near Montreal, for example, have become famous for their skill in the construction of skyscrapers. People on the sidewalks of New York, Chicago, and Boston have stood for hours, their eyes focused on the dizzying heights above, as the Mohawk workers piece together and weld the steel girders of the man-made towers.

Not all status Indians live on reserves. Many, primarily those in the North, have not yet signed land settlement agreements. They still live on and claim ownership of their ancestral lands. These lands include most of the vast Canadian North.

**Non-status Indians.** Because of the legal definition of "Indians" in the Indian Act and the haphazard way in which earlier generations of native people were registered with the government, many native people today find themselves not legally recognized as such by the government. They are not covered by the Indian Act. They have no official status or rights with respect to native land claims. They also have no legal right to claim a share in the privileges of a reserve. They see this as an injustice, and demand official recognition as native people, with the privileges that recognition would bring.

**Métis.** The Métis are in a similar position. Originally the offspring of mixed Indian and European parents, they are also outside the Indian Act. Even though they have no official recognition as native people in the eyes of the law, they too insist that the government acknowledge their special status as native people.

**Inuit.** Finally there are the Inuit (Eskimo) people of Canada's far North. This fourth group is clearly a different people. They have different ancestral origins than any of the other native groups. Like the status Indians, however, the Inuit have special legal status in law. Most Inuit land claims also still remain to be settled.

The traditional Inuit way of life is gradually giving way to the force of change. Like many native people, some Inuit find the changes difficult. Others thrive. Some, for instance, have welcomed employment with the oil and gas companies exploring the Arctic region. Still others have turned traditional Inuit crafts to profit. Authentic Inuit painting and sculpture have become very popular in Canada and the United States. Inuit artist cooperatives have become successful in marketing their work to appreciative buyers.

Sun Owl *by Kenjouak. Cape Dorset.*

Spirit Mask,
*18th century, Central Arctic.*

Eskimo Holding his Hair *by Kabowakotu, Cape Dorset.*

**Land settlements.** Some issues involving native people are well beyond the point of simple discussion. Debate over native land claims in Canada today is more than an argument about who owns which large areas of land and how much the land is worth. Most Canadians agree that it is the right of native people to protect or get adequate compensation for land they see as theirs. However, the land the native people see as theirs is sometimes seen by the larger Canadian community as a valuable national asset that must be developed for the good of the national economy.

The native people protest that what others see as open empty land is home to many native people. Their way of life still depends on the land. They reject wholesale exploitation of their environment. They resent outside intrusion all the more if the land in question was never officially granted by treaty. In that case, the battle over land use can be very bitter.

**The case of James Bay.** The James Bay region of Quebec provides a case in point. In April, 1971, the premier of Quebec addressed 5,000 of his excited supporters at a rally in Montreal. Under a banner proclaiming "The future begins today," he unveiled plans for the massive development of hydro-electric power resources in Quebec's James Bay area.

The development scheme was breathtaking in scope. By rerouting and damming rivers, the government hoped to double Quebec's output of electricity. Much of it would eventually be sold to the power-short northeastern United States. As many as 125,000 jobs would be created in construction, engineering, and manufacturing. It promised to be a boon to Quebec's economy, its exports, and its prestige.

The James Bay development area is enormous. It is larger than Switzerland, Portugal, Belgium, Holland, Denmark, and Luxembourg put together. Almost forgotten in the plan, however, was that the region is home

*Construction moves ahead at James Bay.*

to 6,000 Cree and Inuit. Nobody consulted them. They never signed a treaty relinquishing their land claims. Indeed, until the James Bay announcement was made and construction began, these natives still lived on the land much as their fathers and grandfathers had done for generations.

Progress for Quebec meant much native land would be flooded under huge man-made lakes. It threatened to disrupt ancient trap lines and drive off the geese and caribou the natives hunted for food. It would destroy the spawning grounds for the fish they relied on as part of their diet. For the natives of James Bay, the cost of progress was high. It would cost them their way of life.

Efforts to find a quick compromise failed. The native people wanted all plans for the project stopped until their land claims had been settled. The government of Quebec claimed that in its view the native people had no legal title to the land. The native people, of course, claimed they did. The issue went to court. It was ruled that the native people did have legitimate and direct interest in the land.

With a court ruling against them, the Quebec government was forced to negotiate seriously with the native people of James Bay. Eventually, an agreement was reached. The native people were given legal title to vast areas of land. The project was scaled down to protect other areas from environmental damage. Large cash payments were made, as well as guarantees of future cash payments and social assistance.

161

The James Bay settlement is important. It has become a precedent for others to follow. No longer can native land rights be trampled over in the rush to develop the Canadian interior. The native people's legitimate rights to their land has been upheld in court. No matter how great the desire of other Canadians for the resources of Canada's North, if no prior land settlement exists with local native people, then a settlement must come first.

Today there are extensive development plans for the North, for the British Columbia interior, for the potentially oil-rich and gas-rich Arctic areas. Thousands of jobs and billions of dollars in investment, exports, and manufacturing are at stake.

So, too, is the survival of the native people in these regions. Most Canadians see development as crucial to the country's progress. The native people fear it may destroy their unique way of life. How these land issues will be resolved will be a test of the Canadian commitment to justice and the rights of minorities. For the native people, the land issue, among others, will determine how they will survive as a people.

**The French heritage.** The arrival of French and British settlers in North America began countless generations after the native people had already forged a complex and diverse pattern of life across North America. The coming of these two groups was not without conflict. We have already reviewed the expansion of the French and British colonies. We have noted the rivalry over furs and agricultural lands. We have considered the spillover of European wars into North America. Those wars eventually led to the British takeover of New France and, shortly thereafter, to the independence of the United States. American nationhood, in turn, brought the Loyalists to Canada.

The Loyalists and earlier settlers from Britain were largely English-speaking and Protestant. But whatever plans and hopes they had for a united British North America, they always took French Canadians into account. Who could ignore a large Roman Catholic French-speaking population that showed no interest in giving up its roots? On the contrary, although surrounded on all sides by an English Protestant world, French Canadians were determined to survive. They battled to keep their culture alive. They carefully protected their language, their Church, the education of their children, and their largely agricultural way of life from the outside influence of both English Canada and the United States.

The enduring will of French Canada to survive and flourish has remained a dominant feature of Canadian life. It still shapes the social, political, and institutional life of Quebec. It dominates relations between Quebec and the rest of Canada. It helps to form the Canadian identity.

It would be wrong, however, to oversimplify the English-French issue in Canada. Canada is not one country housing two separate and bickering people — one with roots in France, the other in England. That image may have been valid in the distant past. It certainly is not true today.

French Canada is no satellite of France. It was cut off from France and any large-scale French influence almost 200 years ago, when the British conquered Quebec. As a result, French Canadians experienced neither the French Revolution nor the Napoleonic era. Instead, they have undergone more than 200 years of separate development. They learned early and well to rely on their own resources, their own inspiration, and the warmth of their own traditions to ensure French-Canadian survival within Canada. They have succeeded.

*The rush is on for Canada.*

**The British heritage.** For English-speaking Protestant settlers, the issue of French Canada remained a constant dilemma. How was it possible to fashion a common destiny in a land populated by two distinct founding peoples? There also remained the problem of how to maintain their own distinct identity when they shared so much in common with the Americans to the south.

Throughout their history, Canadians have tried to lessen the impact of the United States on Canadian affairs. They have emphasized Canada's non-American culture and political roots. The French have shown their uniqueness in their determination to survive with their language, religion, and culture intact. For the English before World War II, it was the preservation

164

of links with British tradition and the British Empire that created a sense of separate destiny.

Loyalists and other British settlers felt it their duty to preserve Canada as an outpost of British civilization in North America. Why try to develop a new nation, they argued, when they were already part of a great imperial union, the British Empire? They wanted to retain their British identity, not create a new one. This did not mean that Canada had to be a colony of Britain. Rather, it was hoped that the country would evolve into a full and independent partner of Britain within the British Empire.

Canadians who celebrated their British heritage felt themselves different from Americans. They steadfastly defended the British way of life in North America. In 1776, Americans had fought a war to be free of the British Empire. Canadians chose instead to cherish their connection with it. Even when Canada achieved self-government in 1867, the country retained the Union Jack, the monarchy, the British legal system, and a strong sense of the value of British traditions. Perhaps most important, no matter how similar English-speaking Canadians and Americans appeared, Canadians *felt* themselves different. English Canadians were British.

What role did they see, then, for the culture immigrants brought with them? Before World War II, they saw no room for it at all. Immigrants were expected to become British. Instead of sharing their old-world traditions, they were encouraged to discard them or restrict them to the privacy of their homes.

But immigrants did not live their lives to please others. If their cultures and traditions helped them to ease the difficult process of resettlement, they kept them. They handed them on to their children. Their refusal to turn their backs on their past would eventually lead to a new Canadian identity.

# Double-check

## Review

1. Why do Canada's native people claim special status within the Canadian family of people?

2. In which part of Canada do the native people make up a sizable portion of the population?

3. What are the four categories of native people in Canada?

4. Which aspects of their culture have French Canadians protected and kept alive?

5. Before World War II, what did it mean to be a Canadian in English Canada?

## Discussion

1. Explain the difference between the American melting pot approach to immigration and the Canadian cultural mosaic. Why do you think Canada chose the mosaic? How do you suppose immigrants have responded to these two approaches?

2. Explain the importance of the James Bay settlement. If you had been the judge, what would your decision have been? Explain why.

3. Why do you think it has been so difficult for English-speaking Canadians to form a unique identity?

## Activities

1. Because of the legal definition of "Indians" in the Indian Act, many native people are not officially recognized by the Canadian government. Students might be interested in reading *Halfbreed*, a story describing the life of a non-status Indian woman. They might then lead a class discussion on the difficulties faced by non-status Indians.

2. Some students might want to research Inuit life in the past. Others might do the same for the present. The two groups might then get together and give a presentation entitled "Inuit Life — Past and Present."

3. French Canadians have worked very hard to keep their culture intact, not only their language and religion, but also their unique French-Canadian cooking. Some students might locate a French-Canadian cookbook and prepare some French-Canadian food to share with the class.

# Skills

## A MODERN CREE LEGEND

Long ago a Whiteman came from across the sea to our land. He spoke to our ancestor, who was sitting on a huge log.

"Move over," said the Whiteman.

Our ancestor moved over a little and the Whiteman sat on the log.

The Whiteman nudged him and again said, "Move over." The Indian moved over a little.

Soon the Whiteman repeated, "Move over." This happened again and again until our ancestor was pushed off the log. Then the Whiteman said, "The log is now mine."

Our ancestor took off his hat and respectfully asked, "May I sit on one small part of the log?"

"No," said the Whiteman, "I am using all of the log. But the stump of the tree is nearby. Why don't you sit on it?"

Since then the Indians have been sitting on the very small stump and hoping that the Whiteman would never want it.

Source: *Indians without Tipis* by Bruce Sealey and Verna Kirness, Book Society, 1974.

*Use the legend above and information in Chapter 12 to answer the following questions.*

1. What is a legend?

2. Where did the "Whiteman" come from in the legend?
   (a) Asia  (b) Australia  (c) Europe

3. What does the "huge log" stand for in the legend?
   (a) the North American continent
   (b) a large ship built out of wood
   (c) the customs and traditions of the native people

4. In the legend, what stands for the reserves where native people were sent to live?
   (a) the ancestor  (b) the tree stump  (c) the end of the log

5. Where do most status Indians live today?

# Chapter 13

# Land of Many Peoples

Every day airplanes from all over the world land at Canada's international airports. They carry thousands of passengers. Some are coming to Canada on business. Others are tourists, excited about their holiday plans. There are also Canadians, returning from trips abroad. And there is another important group, the immigrants. These are people who have decided to resettle permanently in Canada and carve out a new life for themselves.

**The immigration process.** Before passengers can claim their luggage, go through customs examination, and depart from the airport, all must undergo a Canadian immigration inspection. For most, the examination is routine. Each is asked, "What country are you a citizen of?" After showing proper Canadian identification, returning Canadians hurriedly move on to pick up their suitcases. Tourists and business people from abroad show a passport or other identification and are also processed quickly.

But for would-be immigrants, the inspection can

take more time. Since they are coming to live in Canada, they must prove they are eligible for admission under the rules and regulations of Canadian immigration legislation. Most have already been screened abroad. At Canadian immigration offices overseas, Canadian authorities carefully assess all those who apply for permanent admission to Canada. Each is measured against a set of criteria the country demands of immigrants. Age, education, employment opportunities, occupation, health, criminal record, and whether a person has close family in Canada are among the factors today's Canadian immigration authorities take into account. If the individual qualifies, he or she is granted the appropriate documents for admission.

Each new immigrant is considered a "New Canadian." Like millions who entered Canada earlier, New Canadians become eligible for Canadian citizenship after three years of living in the country. Then they swear an oath of allegiance to Canada and become Canadian citizens. They are no different in the eyes of the law from people born in Canada.

**Developing an immigration policy.** For many years, Canada was interested in encouraging the "right type" of immigrant to settle there — in particular, English-speaking Protestants from Britain. Such a policy made economic sense. Immigrants filled empty land. They created a market for Canadian manufactured goods. Their skills developed the Canadian economy.

Scottish, Welsh, and Protestant Irish settlers were encouraged to come as well. English-speaking Canadians were confident that these settlers could be counted on to help keep the spirit of British civilization alive. Americans who were prepared to pledge allegiance to the British crown were also welcomed. These settlers were especially prized for their experience in agriculture and industry.

*New arrivals, tired but eager for a better life.*

*Lunch break in a logging camp.*

*Evidence of success.*

While Canada wanted immigrants, that country was second choice for many of the people looking for new homes. Large numbers of settlers chose the United States. It often appeared a more exciting, prosperous, and progressive land of opportunity.

**The Irish.** In the late 1840's, Canada began to attract settlers who were not Protestant and often not English speaking. The first major wave was the Catholic Irish. And they were more than just first. They established both a pattern of settlement and a pattern of response from other Canadians.

The Irish immigration began when overpopulated Ireland suffered a tragic failure of its potato harvest. Potatoes were a staple food item in the Irish diet. Famine spread. Rather than starve, many Irish were forced to abandon their homes to build new lives abroad. Large numbers turned to Canada.

These New Canadians were different from any Canada had seen before. While some spoke English, others did not. What is more, the majority were not necessarily loyal to the British crown. Indeed, the Catholic Irish had a reputation for rebellion against the British.

They also came with few resources except their dreams of the future and their willingness to work. Work they did. Some took up farming and Irish rural communities grew. Many found work as laborers in the cities. Canadian towns and cities developed Irish sections or wards. Others found seasonal labor outside the towns. They dug the new shipping canals, cut trees in the lumbering camps, or laid track for the first railway lines. This type of work often meant weeks or months away from home. Their wives and children stayed behind.

The Catholic Irish filled the bottom rung of the social ladder. Most were poor, and their style of life seemed very different from that of the established community. Many of the men labored far from home for much of the year. That made them seem rootless in the eyes of other Canadians.

As a result, the Irish suffered harsh discrimination. Canada was prepared to use Irish muscle, but it feared and resented the Irish ways. As the number of Irish immigrants grew, some Canadians condemned them as clannish. They resented what seemed like an unwillingness to adopt a Protestant British way of life.

**Foreign labor.** After Confederation, many Irish immigrants found work on the construction of the Canadian Pacific Railway. But there were not enough of them. The railway's appetite for labor seemed endless. Work gangs were brought in from the United States. Even this could not fill the demand. Soon it became necessary to recruit workers from southern and eastern Europe. To build the railway inland from the Pacific, thousands of additional laborers were brought from China.

Most of these laborers were not true immigrants. They were not encouraged to settle in Canada. There were few women and families among them. They came as migrants. They came to earn money to meet the needs of their families at home. When their work was done, they were expected to leave. Most did.

But some did not. Those few who remained behind found other work. Eventually, many married in Canada or sent for wives and families from abroad. These non-British settlers became the forerunners of tens of thousands of others who settled permanently in Canada after the transcontinental railway was completed. They changed the face of Canada forever. They eventually changed the very definition of what it meant to be a Canadian.

**Controlled mass immigration.** A new wave of immigration began at the turn of the century. The railroad had opened the Canadian interior to settlement. Soon there was a rising world demand for Canadian wheat.

The government recognized the opportunity and moved immediately to fill the West with settlers. The result was an encouragement of mass immigration.

Clifford Sifton, the aggressive Minister of the Interior, initiated a far-reaching program to promote Canadian immigration. Unabashedly colonial, the government defined most immigrants who did not come from Britain as "foreign." The one exception was those coming from the United States. Sifton drew up plans to fill the Canadian prairies with wealthy British and American farmers.

Government policy mirrored the views of other nationalities that most Canadians held during that period. Sifton, however, added a new element to the immigration program. He began to admit agricultural settlers from central and eastern Europe. He looked not only for male migrant laborers, but for families. As he explained, "I think a stalwart peasant in a sheepskin coat, born on the soil, whose forefathers have been farmers for ten generations, with a stout wife and a half-dozen children is good quality."

Powerful business and railroad interests were pressing him for even more people. There were large tracts of land to sell in western Canada. In addition, there were large profits to be made from the sale of Canadian wheat. Sifton and his officials were prepared to set aside their prejudices in their frantic search for farmers.

British and American settlers were still their first choice. But if more could not be found, they needed substitutes. Their second choice were Scandinavians, Germans, and other Northern Europeans. Then came Ukrainians, Russians, and Poles. Close to the bottom of the list came those who were, in the government's mind, less desirable people. These included Jews, Italians, South Slavs, Greeks, and Syrians. At the very bottom came blacks and Asians.

*Clifford Sifton set out to fill the West with farmers.*

Hundreds of thousands of farmers from across central and eastern Europe were recruited before the outbreak of World War I. Peasant farmers from the Ukraine, Hungary, Russia, and Poland joined almost a million Americans who had moved north, and Canadians who had gone west by rail. These people made the Canadian West one of the world's most important agricultural regions.

**Discrimination.** Not all settlers were equally welcome. Some were not encouraged to come. Others were excluded.

Negro slaves from the United States had seen Canada as a beacon of hope and freedom in the days before the American Civil War. They had made their way along the "Underground Railway" to freedom in Canada. At the turn of the century, however, the Canadian public wanted no more. Similarly, they wanted no more Asians once the transcontinental railway was finished.

*Prejudice and hostility faced unsuspecting immigrants.*

The entry of Asians and blacks was restricted. In 1910 and 1911, for example, rumors spread that a group of American blacks was preparing to migrate to central Alberta. They were descendants of freed American slaves living in the Oklahoma territory. They had been granted farm land and had hoped to build new lives. Gradually the white population of Oklahoma increased. New settlers soon dominated the Oklahoma legislature and enacted discriminatory laws. The blacks were disheartened and discouraged. For some, the idea of living in Canada seemed a good one. As a result, several families moved north to Alberta.

Rumors spread that a mass migration of blacks was likely. Whites in Alberta reacted quickly and strongly against such a migration. Federal authorities were soon under pressure to close the border to all blacks.

There was nothing in the Canadian Immigration Act to specifically bar black Americans. There was, however, enough leeway to deny entry to any would-be immigrant for health reasons. The government merely instructed immigration inspectors along the border to reject all blacks as unfit for admission on medical

176

grounds. It went even further. It placed advertisements in U.S. newspapers declaring that all blacks would be refused admission to Canada for medical reasons. Blacks were warned not to waste time and money planning to immigrate. All but a few were kept out.

Similar steps were taken to restrict the entry of other groups.

**Urban immigration.** Many thousands of southern and eastern European immigrants were allowed to settle on the Canadian prairies, so long as they were willing to work hard and live on farms. They were also welcome to work in the mines and forests of the interior.

Not all immigrants were content with rural life, however. Many Jews, Italians, Macedonians, Poles, Ukrainians, Russians, and Finns chose instead to work and live in cities. In Montreal, Winnipeg, Toronto, Hamilton, and Vancouver, they awakened all the anxieties and prejudices that had previously been reserved for the Irish.

*Immigrants worked tirelessly to lay Toronto's streetcar tracks.*

Some Canadians responded to the newcomers in their midst with a dignified tolerance. They recognized that their labor and skill were necessary. Immigrants, they realized, earned their keep. They were the ones who laid streetcar tracks, labored in the expanding clothing industry, and tunneled under cities to create modern sewer systems. If immigrant living conditions were poor, tolerant Canadians knew they could and would improve. They also had faith that, with education, immigrants and their children would accept a more British way of life.

Unfortunately, to other Canadians these immigrants were indeed "foreigners" speaking strange languages. They were subjects of czars and kaisers. Their religions and customs seemed out of place. What, these Canadians worried, would become of the Canadian way of life if the foreign influx continued? Soon there was a shrill demand for further restriction of immigration.

**The door closes.** By the mid 1920's, the declining need for agricultural settlers in western Canada and the hostility toward immigrants in the city had their effect. Canada's doors gradually closed. With the mass unemployment of the Great Depression during the 1930's, the doors were locked.

While that may have made good economic sense, it was a human tragedy. In the midst of the Depression, Hitler and the Nazis took power in Germany. Hitler was determined to be rid of the Jews by whatever means was necessary. Canada, like the other western democracies, refused to admit all but a tiny handful of those unfortunate people. If the democracies would not take them, Hitler felt free to deal with them as he wished. Six million Jews and six million others Hitler judged undesirable were systematically and mercilessly put to death. Canada, no less than the other western democracies, must share responsibility for those events.

**Modern day immigration.** Renewed prosperity and labor shortages in the postwar period reopened the doors to immigration. But post World War II immigration was different. Canada was now a major urban industrial power. Immigrants were directed into urban industries or technologically advanced rural industry. Canada took in thousands of industrial, technical, and professional workers.

Another important change was also taking place. As a result of the horror the Nazis had inflicted, Canada slowly moved to stamp out discrimination. Racism and prejudice toward "foreigners" was vigorously attacked. It was also gradually weeded out of Canadian immigration procedures.

When immigration reopened in the postwar period, British settlers were the first to arrive. Soon the way was cleared for the admission of people from all over Europe. Many were displaced persons who had survived the Nazi years. They were followed by others fleeing Communism. After the 1956 Hungarian uprising, more than 30,000 Hungarians fled to Canada. In 1967, thousands of Czechs were admitted after an uprising against the Russians failed in Czechoslovakia.

*In London, England — one of many around the world.*

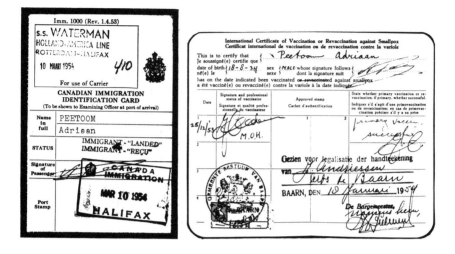

Not all the political dissidents were from behind the Iron Curtain. During the Vietnam War, Canada gave sanctuary to an estimated 10,000 U.S. draft resisters. Many returned to the United States when they received amnesty. Others stayed to become Canadian citizens. They, like other immigrants from throughout the world, had found a new homeland.

Political refugees have formed but a part of recent Canadian immigration. The demand for labor and special skills brought Italians, Greeks, Portuguese, and others by the thousands. Soon they were bringing brothers, sisters, aunts, and uncles over from the old country. New immigrant neighborhoods sprang up in most major Canadian cities. The face of Canada was changing.

More recently, Asian and black immigration has made its mark. Chinese from Hong Kong, Jews from the Soviet Union, Sikhs from India, blacks from the Caribbean, Latin Americans escaping poverty and civil strife, and Vietnamese boat people have all found new homes in Canada. The ethnic and racial color bars have finally been eliminated. Today, almost one-third of Canada's population is neither French nor British in origin.

**A new identity for Canada.** After the war, the long-standing British Canadian identity gradually faded. With the emerging independence of its colonies, the British Empire was replaced by the British Commonwealth. The Commonwealth represented a new model of international cooperation. But without the old ties, what would be the binding identity of English-speaking Canada?

French-Canadian identity remained secure within a long cultural tradition. Modern Quebec, like the rest of Canada, became more urban and more secular. But the strength of French-Canadian individuality was not diminished.

Nor was French Canada alone in asserting its cultural muscle. As we have seen, before World War II, New Canadians were subject to attempts to make them British. Many resented the effort. In spite of the pressure, they clung to the warmth of their own cultures and traditions. All the while, they contributed to the growth of Canada. They fought side by side with other Canadians in the war. They proved their loyalty and dedication many times over. Why then, they asked, should they and their families be made to feel like second-class citizens? Their cultures and traditions were no less worthy than those of other Canadians. They were ready to become English-speaking Canadians, but not British. In the postwar period, they asserted their right to full and equal participation in Canadian society.

The federal government responded with human rights laws that eliminated racial and ethnic discrimination. It also reaffirmed the equality of French and English as the two official languages. No one expected all Canadians to become bilingual. But it was recognized that all were entitled to official services in either language.

*Typical ethnic events.*

**Multiculturalism.** In 1971, the federal government recognized the contributions of all Canada's cultural communities. All traditions were recognized as contributing to the greater strength of the country. No longer would New Canadians be encouraged to part with their heritage in order to be "real" Canadians. Just the opposite. It was hoped that all Canadians would find strength and richness in their country's diversity. Canada has two official languages. It also has a mosaic of culturally equal streams. The mosaic, now called multiculturalism, has become government policy.

This vision of a multicultural Canada is not accepted by all Canadians. Old ways die hard. Some are still faithful to a British image. They are concerned lest their vision of Canada be swept aside by this multicultural ideal. Some in French Canada, who rightly see themselves as a Canadian founding people, do not want to become just one among many ethnic cultures. The native people remain uneasy over their place in the mosaic. Others wonder whether the emphasis on multiculturalism, like regional differences, will prevent the gradual evolution of a single Canadian identity.

These concerns are not easily dismissed. They continue as part of a democratic society's efforts to chart its way into the future. What shape Canada — regionally diverse, bilingual, multi-ethnic — will take in the future remains to be seen. Whether a multicultural vision of the country will take deep root or be replaced by another we cannot know. But the debate involves all of its 25 million people. It is a measure of Canada's strength and deep commitment to justice for all its citizens.

# Double-check

## Review

1. After how many years do New Canadians become eligible for Canadian citizenship?

2. From which countries were settlers encouraged to come in the beginning?

3. Which people were the first major group of "foreign" immigrants?

4. During what years was the Canadian immigration door closed?

5. How has Canadian immigration policy changed since World War II?

## Discussion

1. Each immigrant accepted by Canada today is called a "New Canadian." In Clifford Sifton's day, these same people were called "foreigners." What does this change in terminology reflect?

2. For many people looking for new homes, Canada was second choice; the United States was first. Why do you think that was true? Is it still true today? Explain your opinion.

3. Closing the immigration door in the 1930's made good economic sense, but it was a human tragedy. Discuss this viewpoint.

## Activities

1. Students might write for the booklet entitled "The Canadian Citizen" (Citizenship Registration, 55 St. Clair Ave. E., Toronto, Ontario M4T 1M2) to find out about the Canadian citizenship process. They might try to answer the questions that applicants have to be able to answer.

2. Students might do some research and write a report about a recent refugee group that has taken shelter in Canada: for instance, the Hungarians, the Russian Jews, the Vietnamese boat people, or the U.S. draft dodgers.

3. Many blacks from the United States went to Canada before the American Civil War, some to Ontario (the town Tom escaped to in *Uncle Tom's Cabin* still exists in Ontario), others to Nova Scotia. Some students might want to find out about the Underground Railway and the Canadians who helped slaves escape to freedom.

# Skills

## IMMIGRATION TO CANADA: 1867 to 1980

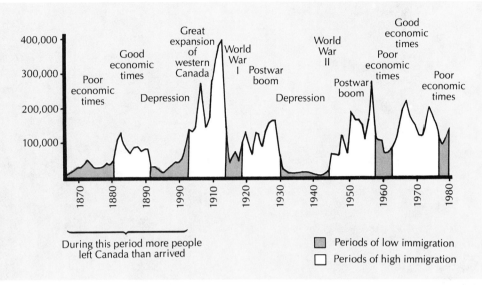

Source: *Canada: Land of Diversity,*
Prentice-Hall, 1983.

*Use the graph above and Chapter 13 to answer the following questions.*

1. What do the light-colored parts of the graph represent?
   (a) periods of poor economic times
   (b) periods of high immigration
   (c) periods of expansion

2. Look at the periods of low immigration on the graph. Name one reason for these periods of low immigration.

3. During what period did Canada have the highest immigration?

4. What were some reasons for such high immigration?

5. In general, how does immigration seem to be related to the economic times?

# 6
# TODAY'S
# CHALLENGES

Chapter 14

# The New Constitution, Regionalism and the English/French Debate

On July 1, 1967, Queen Elizabeth was in Canada to proclaim a year of celebration. It was Canada's Centennial. Exactly one hundred years earlier, the present Queen's great-grandmother, Queen Victoria, had signed the British North America Act to make Canada a self-governing country.

The Canadian mood in 1967 was festive. After a century of growth and development, it seemed that all Canadians were united in celebration. Everywhere a party spirit was in the air. Montreal led off with Expo 67, a world's fair the likes of which had never been seen before. In every city, town, and village, Canadians developed their own Centennial projects. Each one provided another expression of pride in Canada and gratitude for all that Canada meant to its citizens. Canadians looked to the past with pride and to the future with confidence.

According to many, Montreal's Expo 67 was
the best World's Fair ever.

Nevertheless, even as they joined in saluting their
country's Centennial, Canadians could not ignore the
fact that certain challenges remained to be solved.
Some problems were as old as Canada, or older. One of
the outstanding questions was the British North America Act itself. The BNA Act was passed by the British
parliament in London. It proclaimed the confederation
of British colonies in North America, which created
Canada. It also detailed the rights and responsibilities
of the federal and provincial governments.

Though the BNA Act was the basis of Canada's
system of government, it was not Canadian legislation.
It was British. Canada, many Canadians felt, should
have its own home-made constitution to replace the
BNA Act. This, they argued, would be the last step on
the country's long journey from colony to independent
nation.

**A Canadian Constitution.** On April 17, 1982, the
Queen visited Canada again. With all the pomp of a
royal occasion, she and various Canadian representatives gathered on Parliament Hill in Ottawa to sign a
new Canadian-made Constitution. A crowd of thousands roared their approval and a 21-gun salute boomed
in the background. Canada's new Constitution, with

its Charter of Rights and Freedoms, was proclaimed the supreme law of Canada. After more than 100 years of self-government, Canadians had their own Constitution, one that also enshrined in law the basic freedoms and rights the people enjoyed.

Why had it taken more than 100 years for Canadians to write their own constitution? They had tried several times earlier, but had failed. The federal and provincial governments could not agree amongst themselves. Each was concerned that a new constitution might reduce its own powers. Nor could they work out a formula for amending a constitution once it was proclaimed. Instead of wasting time in endless arguments, Canada's leaders had simply made do with the BNA Act. If there was to be a Canadian-made constitution, it would be up to a future generation to write it.

The future finally arrived. It was time for new and bold leaders to make the necessary compromises. Hard, sometimes bitter negotiations between the federal government and the provinces began in earnest. In 1982, after several years of discussion, the provisions were finally hammered out. The new Constitution was proclaimed.

It marked a new beginning. A constitution, after all, is more than just words written on parchment. It is more than just a document to be preserved in a glass case for tourists to see when they visit Ottawa. It is a living document. The Canadian Constitution and its important Charter of Rights and Freedoms are now the foundation of Canadian law. They contain the rules by which Canadians agree to build their society. From now on, they will provide the guiding principles for dealing with important Canadian issues.

The United States has had its own Constitution and Bill of Rights for more than 200 years. As a result, Americans today take constitutional review of legislation by the courts for granted. It is different for Canada. Canadians are still unsure what their new Constitution and its Charter of Rights and Freedoms will mean when applied to Canadian issues. Canadian courts are only now beginning to interpret this new, most important law.

*Many crucial decisions will be made in this building in the next few years.*

**The Canadian challenge.** Herein lies the challenge. The Canadian Constitution is new, but many of Canada's problems are not. Most grow out of three ongoing Canadian concerns. Firstly, there is the need to create national harmony in a country with such diverse regional, cultural, economic, and language differences. Secondly, there is the challenge of charting an independent Canadian course while living peacefully alongside the world's most powerful and influential nation, the United States. Thirdly, there is the need to ensure the economic growth of Canada for the benefit of Canadians.

What, Canadians wonder, will their new Constitution mean when applied to these concerns? Can it assist them in achieving their national goals? Will it help them to find a new beginning as they strive to resolve their difficulties? It is still too early to answer these questions. But, so we can better understand Canada today, let us explore the issues that now occupy the minds of Canadians. Let us attempt to understand the challenge these issues represent for Canadians.

**Regionalism.** Canada's history and geography have encouraged the development of regional differences and local loyalties. Each of its seven distinct regions has its own character, its own interests, and its own concerns.

The island province of Newfoundland is isolated from the rest of Canada by both water and tradition. It was the last province to join Confederation, in 1949. Local sentiment is still so strong that the people continue to refer to themselves as Newfoundlanders and to those on the mainland as Canadians. Even now, they retain a deep sense of local tradition and separate historical development. Much like the people of the American South, over time Newfoundlanders developed a local accent and vocabulary. It is as distinct to the ears of other English Canadians as the accent of those from Mississippi or Alabama is to Americans elsewhere in the country.

Although the provinces of Nova Scotia, New Brunswick, and Prince Edward Island are each different from the others, the Maritime region retains a special character binding Maritimers together and setting them off from other Canadians. The area is rich in the history of early colonial settlement. British and French settlers were drawn to the region by fertile farmlands, and more especially, by good fishing waters. The sea shaped the Maritime character. But the region has been burdened by lack of economic opportunity and poverty. Today, economic hopes are again pinned on the Atlantic. The promise of large-scale offshore Atlantic oil production has become a flag of financial hope.

Canada's largest single province, Quebec, is synonymous with French Canada. Here, as we have already learned, the historical struggle to keep the French Canadian language and culture alive since the conquest has instilled in Quebecers a deep-seated feeling for their province. Indeed, for many it is more than a province. Quebec is their homeland, with a special flavor all its own.

Ontario is the wealthy industrial region of Canada. It is heavily populated, and dominated by big cities radiating out into ever-expanding suburbs. In 1984, Ontario celebrated the 200th anniversary of its first settlement by the Loyalists. The spirit of Ontario in the last 25 years has been shaped by rapid growth and constant change. The province has been a magnet, drawing in new industries and hundreds of thousands of people from other parts of Canada and around the world to meet the needs of its economic explosion.

Further west is the Prairie region of western Canada — Manitoba, Saskatchewan, and Alberta. Many Westerners resent what they see as the economic power of distant Ontario. The prairie economy is based largely on wheat farming and raw resources. Both have often required investment capital and loans from the Ontario money market. Some Westerners also feel that import tariffs force them to purchase expensive Ontario manufactured goods when cheaper imported items are available. As a result, many people on the prairies feel that prosperous Ontario has treated them like poor cousins. That province, they argue, has grown wealthy on prairie economic trials. While these feelings may be exaggerated, they add to the Prairie region's sense of community.

On the Pacific coast, British Columbia is a region all its own. It too has recently mushroomed in population, particularly in the Vancouver area. But the special regional quality of British Columbia has less to do with its recent urban growth than with its physical isolation from the rest of Canada. Here amidst the majestic beauty of its natural setting, people are drawn to the outdoors both for pleasure and for the wealth of natural resources.

The last Canadian region is also its largest — the Canadian North. In this sparsely populated vastness, Northerners are drawn together by a common sense of being part of Canada's, and North America's, last great frontier. Local history is filled with the traditions and folkways of the native people, who make up a large part of the population. But Northerners seem less concerned with the past than with the future. It is with an eye to the future that Canada's northern regional character is taking shape.

The different regions of Canada and their regional loyalties have been an issue since the compromises of Confederation. In any attempt to build a common Canadian identity, regionalism has always been an important factor.

**Bilingual Canada.** The Canadian coat of arms shows Canada's national crest flanked on the left by a majestic lion and on the right by a stately unicorn. The lion, holding a Union Jack, represents Canada's British roots. The unicorn, holding a *fleur-de-lis*, represents the French tradition.

Canada is a bilingual country. Whatever language might be spoken in the privacy of a Canadian home, or between members of the same ethnic group, all Canadians share in the use of English and French as the languages of public communication. The two languages are recognized as equal in the workings of commerce and government.

The coexistence of two quite different cultural and language traditions has been crucial in the unfolding of Canada's history. It remains among the most important challenges Canadians face. In the past, relations between English-speaking and French-speaking Canadians have not always been harmonious. Echoes of this often troubled relationship still sound through Canadian society.

Two issues stand out for special consideration. Firstly, there is the relationship of the province of Quebec with the rest of Canada. Secondly, there are the problems concerning language rights of both French-speaking minorities in primarily English-speaking Canada and English-speaking minorities in French-speaking Quebec.

**The Quiet Revolution in Quebec.** Quebec remains the heart of French-speaking Canada. The past few decades have ushered in enormous changes there. Approximately 80 percent of Quebecers can trace their roots back to the French colony of New France. But gone are the days when Quebec was neatly divided between a French-speaking Catholic rural population and a smaller urban English-speaking group concentrated in Montreal. Today much of the province's population has shifted into the cities. Other changes have also taken place. There has been increased immigration from abroad, a decline in the influence of the Roman Catholic Church, a sharp fall in the birth rate, mass public education, and industrialization. The impact of all these changes has been so dramatic and far-reaching that they have been called the "Quiet Revolution."

An important part of the Quiet Revolution has been political. In the 1950's, Quebec's French majority slowly but firmly asserted control over all aspects of life in the province. Among the most important recent moves was the official removal of English as the language of business, commerce, and government. English was replaced with French. This, French Canadians hoped, would open the door for French-speaking Quebecers to move into top positions in business and government. These positions had been the virtual monopoly of the minority English-speaking community.

To ensure the prime position of the French language in Quebec, the government made French-language study compulsory even in English-language schools. Immigrants from abroad could previously choose whether their children went to French-language or English-language schools. Now all immigrants and their Canadian-born children have no choice. They must go to French schools. Even the use of English on street signs and billboards has been banned. Signs are in French only. If Quebec is to remain part of Canada, the government is determined it will be as a French-speaking province.

There were those Quebecers, largely English-speaking, for whom the language changes were too much. Since they could not speak French, they felt isolated. They feared their opportunity to earn an adequate income would be lessened. They increasingly felt like strangers in their own province. They were also worried that their English-speaking children would be denied the opportunity of a full and equal life in French-speaking Quebec. For some of these English-speaking Quebecers, a move to English Canada solved their difficulties. The majority, however, are committed to carving a place for themselves in the new Quebec. Many are learning French.

If Quebec's French-language laws went too far for some, they did not go far enough for others. These people, called "separatists," believe that Quebec will never be truly French so long as it remains the only French-speaking province in a confederation of ten.

*The musical sawyer is Rene Levesque, premier of Quebec.*

*Newspaper headlines proclaim the FLQ crisis in 1970.*

They want Quebec to become a country of its own. They want independence from the rest of Canada. For a time in the late 1960's and early 1970's, a tiny minority of radicals were prepared to use violence to promote their cause. But in October, 1970, the federal government, fearing open rebellion, used the Canadian military to crush the small group.

The vast majority of Quebec separatists, however, reject violence as a tool in their effort to take Quebec out of Canada. They hope to win independence by democratic means. In 1976, a democratic separatist political party, the Parti Quebecois, won the Quebec provincial election. It was re-elected in 1981.

*By law, all labels must contain both official languages.*

Surprisingly, the election of this separatist party did not bring independence for Quebec. In 1980, the province held a vote on independence. All Quebecers, both English-speaking and French-speaking, were asked their opinion about establishing an independent Quebec. Odd as it may seem, after electing a separatist government into power, the people of Quebec overwhelmingly voted "No" to the separation of Quebec from Canada.

For the immediate future, it seems that Quebecers have chosen to remain part of the Canadian Confederation. Whether the province will stay in Confederation or someday move toward independence, we cannot know. The vast majority of Canadians, including a majority of those in Quebec, hope it will find its place in Canada. Most are willing to work toward this end, even if it means some sacrifice by all Canadians.

**French outside Quebec.** Quebec is not the only home of French-speaking Canadians. There are large and important French Canadian communities in New Brunswick, Ontario, and Manitoba. But they remain minorities.

Those French communities pose a special challenge to the provinces in which they are found. They want provincial government services to be provided in French. They mean such things as French-language schools, the use of French in courts, and the publication of all provincial documents in French as well as English.

The French-speaking minorities point out that Canada is officially a bilingual country. The federal government makes every effort to ensure that federal services — such things as income-tax forms and postal services — are available to all Canadians in the official language of their choice. For example, with financial aid from the federal government, both French and English television and radio programs are available to most Canadians, wherever they live.

The federal government's lead has been followed by many in Canada's business community. Companies realize that the majority of people in Quebec, and significant minorities elsewhere, speak French. They want goods and services available in French. By federal law, everything from the writing on breakfast cereal boxes to instructions on how to use the latest home computer are printed in both official languages.

Not all the provinces, however, have followed the federal government's lead. Not all have made an equal commitment to bilingualism. Quebec has traditionally offered all its citizens services in both English and French. As we have seen, it recently changed that policy.

In the rest of Canada, provincial records are equally spotty. New Brunswick, with its important and large French-speaking minority, is officially bilingual. Provincial services, including education from grade school to university, are available in both French and English. Ontario has not gone that far. It offers its French-speaking community a wide range of services in French, including elementary and high school education where numbers warrant. But the province has refused to become officially bilingual.

**The Manitoba case.** Manitoba has an important French-speaking minority that includes the descendants of its original French-speaking Catholic Métis people. When Manitoba entered Confederation in 1870, after the first Métis rebellion, the Métis were promised French language rights and publicly funded Catholic schools. Later the provincial government went back on these guarantees. French language equality and publicly funded Catholic schools were both withdrawn. In spite of protests from French-speaking Catholics, the Manitoba action stood.

Several years ago, a French-speaking Manitoban received a traffic ticket. He went to court and claimed that the ticket he had been issued was invalid. It was, he pointed out, printed only in English. He argued that the terms of Manitoba's entry into Confederation required the province to be officially bilingual. The Manitoba action revoking French language rights, he asserted, was illegal. Since his traffic ticket was an official government document printed only in English, it must be invalid. If he was right, Manitoba was still officially bilingual. To almost everyone's shock, the court agreed. The traffic ticket was ruled invalid.

The issue, of course, was not the single traffic ticket. It was whether or not Manitoba, after all these years, was still officially bilingual. In 1984, the Manitoba government attempted to resolve this larger issue. It was prepared to take a bold step. Calling for equal justice for all its citizens, it proposed bringing forward a law declaring Manitoba bilingual.

The opposition party in the Manitoba provincial assembly led a crusade against the move. The province, they insisted, was English speaking and should stay that way. They were supported by a majority of Manitoba citizens. Those opposed to official bilingualism obviously resented the added cost to the taxpayer. Even more, they feared that in the future the best jobs in government, industry, and education would go to those who were bilingual. This, they worried, would mean that any English-speaking person who wanted to succeed in Manitoba would have to become French speaking. It would create three language groups — an English group, a French group, and an elite bilingual group.

The public protest was so loud, and the attack from the opposition in the Manitoba assembly so strong, that the plan to make the province officially bilingual was withdrawn. The language issue and the case of the traffic ticket have been sent to the Supreme Court of Canada to be resolved.

Not only in Manitoba, but across Canada, tension over conflicting English and French language demands persists. Compromise seems difficult. As both sides claim their cause is right and their demands are just, the new Constitution and the courts will have a tough job cut out for them. The future shape of Canadian society hangs on the outcome of their deliberations.

*Canada's national anthem.*

# Double-check

1. In what year did Canada proclaim its new Constitution and its Charter of Rights and Freedoms?

2. In which region is the economy based almost entirely on wheat farming and natural resources?

3. What was the "Quiet Revolution"?

4. Who are the separatists?

5. Which three provinces, other than Quebec, have large French Canadian communities?

## Discussion

1. Great Britain's constitution is unwritten, based on traditions, practices and beliefs. What is a constitution? What are the advantages and disadvantages of a written constitution? Of an unwritten one?

2. After electing a separatist government, the people of Quebec voted "no" to the separation of Quebec from Canada. Why do you think French Canadians decided against an independent Quebec? In what ways does Quebec need Canada? In what ways does Canada need Quebec?

3. What problems might a province have in becoming officially bilingual? Why do you think New Brunswick has become officially bilingual? Why has Ontario not done so? Do you think this will change? Explain your reasons.

## Activities

1. Students might locate copies of the Canadian Charter of Rights and Freedoms and the American Bill of Rights to compare the two and report on how they are similar and different.

2. To get a feeling of life in one or more of the regions of Canada students might want to read some novels like the following: *The Mountain and the Valley* (about a village in Nova Scotia), *Who Has Seen the Wind* (about prairie life), *Breaking Smith's Quarter Horse* (about ranch life in British Columbia).

3. Two students might prepare a skit in which one English-speaking Quebecker who has moved to Ontario meets another who has stayed in Quebec. They might discuss their lives and the reasons for their different decisions.

# Skills

## USING AN INDEX

Source: *Canada Handbook*, 1984.

*Use the index above and information in Chapter 14 to answer the following questions.*

1. In what order are topics listed in an index?

2. On what pages of the *Canada Handbook* would you find information about citizenship?

3. On how many pages is the House of Commons discussed?

4. On what pages would you find information about the Constitution of Canada?

5. Which pages give information about the BNA Act? Why is the BNA Act given as a subhead under the Constitution?

# Chapter 15

# Canadian/American Relations

A recent prime minister of Canada described the relationship between Canada and the United States as being like a mouse sleeping with a friendly elephant. It can by cozy and warm for the mouse. But the mouse must be careful. There is always danger of being crushed.

Canada's concern about being crushed, economically or culturally, must seem strange to Americans. When they think of Canada, it is likely as a large, friendly neighbor. Millions of Americans carry fond memories of pleasant visits to Canada as tourists. After all, for more than 50 million Americans, Canada is less than one day's drive away. No passport or visa is needed when citizens of either country cross the border into the other.

*Canadian/American relations were never closer than when Ambassador Ken Taylor helped U.S. hostages escape from Iran.*

Many Americans also recall that it was Canadian diplomats who smuggled Americans out of Iran during the 1980 hostage crisis. In recognition of that heroic gesture, Canadian flags were hoisted alongside American flags all over the United States.

Canadian and American flags stand side by side at many sporting events as well. Expo and Blue Jays fans in Montreal and Toronto have enthusiastically embraced the American national pastime of baseball. Similarly, many Americans have come to appreciate Canada's favorite game, hockey. When it comes to hockey and baseball, the Canadian-American border seems irrelevant to players and fans alike.

Good relations between the United States and Canada, however, cannot be taken for granted. On some issues, relations between the two are strained. To understand the Canadian concern, let us look at several points where interests are not the same.

**Cultural competition.** Canadians, especially English-speaking Canadians, are concerned about the American cultural influence on Canada. This is particularly true in the areas of communication and broadcasting. Since most Canadians live close to the border, they have long received a steady diet of U.S. radio and television programming. Now cable television services bring U.S. programming to those more distant from the border. American programming is so popular that Canadian television networks also broadcast U.S. content in order not to lose their Canadian viewers.

Because of the overriding cultural impact of American broadcasting on the Canadian public, quotas for Canadian content were established by the government in 1981. Any television station that does not air a minimum of 50 percent Canadian content will lose its broadcast license. Similarly on radio, even pop music stations are required to broadcast a minimum of 50 percent Canadian content to keep their licenses.

In a free and democratic society, quotas and censorship are not taken lightly. Obviously, the Canadian government feels that the threat to Canadian culture is great. Restrictions on broadcasting of U.S. produced programming underscore their concern about the nation's cultural survival.

*Gordon Sinclair was a well-known Canadian broadcaster and a great admirer of the United States.*

Broadcasting is not the only area of American cultural penetration. Canadian bookstores are stocked with American books. Newsstands carry a wide range of American magazines. Every Hollywood film is screened across English-speaking Canada at the same time as it is in the United States.

Many Canadians feel there should also be regulations restricting these U.S. imports, or at least more encouragement of Canadian culture. It is not that Canadian cultural products are any better or worse than American. It is just, they feel, that Canada must have its own. Canadian talent must be assisted and appreciated at home.

Part of the difficulty in producing Canadian culture is economic. The costs of publishing books, producing films, mounting art exhibits, and staging plays is about the same on both sides of the border. However, the potential Canadian audience is only a fraction of the audience in the United States. As a result, the money available in Canada to support cultural creation is also much less.

Publishing of Canadian books is a case in point. Any book published in the United States has a potential market of almost 250 million readers. If a similar book, in English, is published in Canada, the market is only about 17 million. It is only about eight million if the book is published in French. What is more, Canadian books are not alone on bookstore shelves. American, French, and British books are readily available in Canadian bookstores. Thus, not only must Canadian books compete with one another for the attention of a small book-buying public, they must also compete with imported and often cheaper American books.

**Public support for cultural institutions.** Under such conditions, how can Canadian publishing or other cultural activities survive? Most Canadians reject the idea of restricting the inflow of American books, magazines, film, and art. Nevertheless, they are concerned that their own cultural efforts might be smothered. In order to make Canadian cultural products available, federal and provincial governments use tax dollars in direct support of cultural activities, far more than governments do in the United States. The financial cost of ensuring that Canadian culture will survive is thus carried, in part, by the taxpayer.

Those costs can be high. But, as Canadians will probably agree, the price is worth it. This is especially true for two of the most important Canadian cultural institutions, the Canadian Broadcasting Corporation (CBC) and the National Film Board (NFB). Both were established to ensure the availability of high quality, diverse, and most important, truly Canadian cultural content.

Both were established by the federal government and receive their annual budgets from tax revenue. However, they remain absolutely independent of government control. The Canadian public would not tolerate the government meddling in CBC or NFB productions. Indeed, the CBC and NFB often hold the government up to critical public review through the expert and independent probing of their productions.

The CBC operates separate French and English radio and television networks across Canada. It broadcasts light entertainment, sports, and drama, especially in its television service. The CBC is best known for the high quality of its news and public affairs programs. It offers a unique Canadian view of local issues and major

Canadian
Broadcasting
Corporation

Société
Radio-
Canada

National
Film Board
of Canada

Office
national du film
du Canada

world events. It also helps bind Canadians together as a people, through the free flow of information across the country. CBC programming reaches almost every home in Canada, including those in remote outposts of the Arctic North.

In addition, the CBC promotes the production of Canadian arts. More than any of the competing, privately owned Canadian broadcasters, it has a commitment to Canadian drama, music, and dance. Many Americans living along the Canadian border have learned to appreciate the high quality of CBC television programming, whether entertainment or public affairs. CBC's radio news and public affairs programs have also won a large and loyal U.S. audience. In a rare reversal of the northward flow of most broadcasting, American Public Radio in the United States rebroadcasts many of the popular radio programs to listeners across the United States.

The NFB is the film equivalent of the CBC. It, too, takes special care to reflect honestly the diverse character and concerns of the Canadian community. Among the NFB's accomplishments has been its pioneering of many documentary and short-film techniques we now take for granted. The high quality and often controversial subject matter of NFB productions is world renowned. Year after year, the NFB wins Academy Awards for its films. Today, it is taking a lead in the field of film education. A new and well-prepared band of Canadian film makers will be ready for the challenges of tomorrow.

**Environmental issues.** American culture is not the only thing that flows freely across the border into Canada. So does pollution. This is another area of Canadian concern.

The United States and Canada are both major industrial powers. One of the unpleasant by-products of their mass industrial output has been damage to the environment. Both countries have repeatedly affirmed

their desire to deal with pollution. Each promises to reduce and repair the environmental damage their activities have already caused.

Acid rain is an especially urgent problem. When coal is burned, it sends sulphur emissions into the sky. Cars burning gasoline exhaust nitrogen oxide. When these mix with rain water, they produce an acid that falls to earth in rain or snow. Acid rain is causing billions of dollars worth of damage to the environment. It stunts forests, destroys plant and fish life in lakes and rivers, and destroys the brick and stone face of buildings.

In the past, Canadians have been guilty of producing acid rain. A single smelting smokestack at Sudbury in Ontario's northern mining belt was said to be the worst sulphur polluter in the world. But that era is past. Canada has joined western European countries in pledging to reduce acid rain emissions by a minimum of 30 percent or more before 1993. This is but a first step. The war on acid rain has begun.

But Canada cannot do it alone. It needs the cooperation of the United States. For a 1984 international conference on the acid rain problem, however, the United States refused to send an official delegate. It also refused to endorse the 30 percent clean-up pledge. The problem of acid rain, the United States government argued, needs more study. A clean-up must await the outcome of research.

The problem for Canada is that acid rain falling on eastern Canada comes largely from the United States. Emissions from burning coal, generated especially in the heavily industrial Ohio valley, mix with clouds that float across the border into Canada. This U.S. created acid rain, Canadians charge, is now the chief cause of environmental damage in Canada. Canadians feel they are paying the price for U.S. government indifference to this key environmental crisis. The U.S. government wants years to study the problem. Canadians protest that their lakes and forests are being destroyed today. They accuse the United States of ignoring environmental hazards that directly affect Canada.

The acid rain issue is but one environmental irritant in a growing list. There are others. Chemical waste dumps on the U.S. side of the Great Lakes are leaking dangerously into the water table. Some of the leaking chemicals have been linked to cancer. There are fears that they are gradually seeping into lakes and rivers. Traces are now found in the drinking water of millions of Americans and Canadians. In addition, U.S. irrigation and hydro power projects near the border call for rerouting rivers that flow across the border. This may eventually have devastating effects on fisheries and water quality on the Canadian side.

How the United States and Canada, two friendly neighbors, handle the natural environment that is the birthright of citizens on both sides of their mutual border is critical. It will not only determine the health of millions of Canadians and Americans. It will also set an example for the world to follow. It will show how two neighboring countries can solve their problems in peace.

# Double-check

## Review

1. What American sport has become one of Canada's favorites?

2. How much Canadian content must there be on Canadian radio television and programs?

3. Why is it relatively more expensive to produce Canadian culture than American?

4. Name two important Canadian cultural institutions that are supported by taxpayers.

5. What is acid rain and what damage does it do to the environment?

## Discussion

1. Why does Canada have such close ties with the United States? Do you think such ties are good or bad for Canada? For the United States?

2. Canadian culture is no better and no worse than American, but Canadians feel they must have their own. Why? What is culture? How much do you know about Canadian culture? How might Canada encourage the development of its own culture?

3. Discuss the problem of environmental pollution. What kind of pollution have you experienced? Why must Canada and the United States cooperate in solving this problem? How do you think they should cooperate?

## Activities

1. Students might organize a class display of Canadian cultural products: books, magazines, newspapers, perhaps an NFB documentary film (for a catalog write: National Film Board of Canada, 1251 Avenue of the Americas, 16th Floor, New York, N.Y. 10020), records, tapes, illustrations of Canadian art. They might invite other classes to see their display.

2. Students might locate such Canadian magazines as *Maclean's*, *Saturday Night, Chatelaine*, and *Canadian Living*, or newspapers like *The Globe and Mail* (Toronto), *The Montreal Gazette, The Chronicle-Herald* (Halifax), or *The Vancouver Sun* and read them, paying special attention to the feature stories and the editorials. They might discuss with others what they discover about Canadian life and culture from their reading.

3. Fishing zones and maritime boundaries have become an issue between Canada and the United States because of the decrease in fish stock and because of the future potential of underwater mineral development. Some students might want to find out more about this issue and report to the class.

# Skills

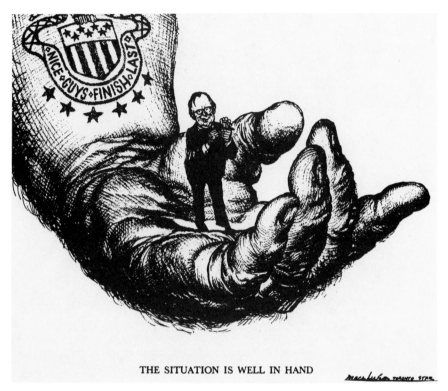

**THE SITUATION IS WELL IN HAND**

Source: The Toronto Star.

*Use the political cartoon and information in Chapter 15 to answer the following questions.*

**1.** Where did the above cartoon appear?

**2.** What country does the hand represent? How do you know?

**3.** What country does the man likely represent?

**4.** The expression "the situation is well in hand" usually means that everything is O.K. Does the cartoon make you feel that everything is O.K.? Explain your answer.

**5.** What might Canadians have thought of this cartoon if it had been drawn by an American?

# Chapter 16

# Canadian Economics

Canada is one of the world's richest nations, with one of the highest standards of living. The country has an abundance of natural resources and its people have the technical skills necessary to use them profitably. It is already a major supplier of raw materials to the world. Minerals, pulp and paper, lumber, food stuffs, and energy resources are exported everywhere.

Canada is a major industrial power. Its factories produce every kind of goods. For instance, the three big automobile manufacturers — General Motors, Ford and Chrysler — each have production plants there. They manufacture cars sold on both sides of the border. Most North American buyers probably have no idea whether the cars they are driving rolled off the assembly line in Canada or in the United States. Perhaps they should not be called "American" cars, but "North American."

Canada is also a world leader in technology. Canadian-built space satellites orbit the globe. The American space shuttle *Challenger,* is equipped with a Canadian-developed, Canadian-built space arm that has been used to launch new satellites into orbit. The space arm was a gift from the people of Canada to the U.S. space program. Canadian scientists experiment in every manner of research. They are involved in medical research, space technology, and computerized and nuclear experimentation. Canadian space astronauts have been trained to join Americans on space missions.

**Keeping pace.** Canada has only a fraction of the population of its major western trading partners, the United States, Britain, and Japan. It is trying to keep up with technological change and industrial development. But this is very expensive. The government has far fewer taxpayers to rely on for support than other major industrial powers do. Canadian businesses have less available money. Keeping pace with modernization is costly. Falling behind, however, would leave the country a second-class power in a changing industrial world. Canadians do not want merely to export raw materials and import manufactured goods.

*Canada's space arm was an important addition to the space-shuttle* Challenger.

To keep pace, Canada must export both its resources and its manufactured goods. This is not too difficult in a period of prosperity. But in a period of recession, when world demand for manufactured goods shrinks and the market for raw materials drops, Canada's economy suffers. This may be true of other countries as well. In Canada, however, with its small population, the domestic market is too small to keep many businesses afloat. Thus, Canada depends more on exports than many other countries do. So, in a world economic slowdown, Canada is hurt somewhat more than its trading partners. High unemployment and economic stagnation become a real threat.

**Regional disparity.** Not all regions or provinces are equally wealthy. Ontario and western Canada are more prosperous than Quebec or the Maritime Provinces. Recent oil and gas finds in the Maritimes may improve the economic prospects for that region.

Canadians have agreed, however, that no part of Canada, whatever its economic condition, should be severely disadvantaged. The wealthier regions must share with the less fortunate. As a result, a complex system of tax sharing between regions exists. Each year the federal government collects taxes from individuals and businesses. It then redistributes a portion of what it collects from the wealthier regions to the less fortunate regions. These transfer payments ensure that all Canadians are guaranteed an acceptable minimum standard of government services and care.

**Public ownership.** Because Canada's economic development has been slow and fragile, Canadian governments have generally been ready to enter the marketplace to stimulate economic growth. In the past, both federal and provincial governments have invested in industrial enterprise and operated businesses regarded as essential to economic strength. The Canadian gov-

*Examples of government owned corporations.*

ernment owns a national railway, the largest Canadian airline, and a radio and television network. It also owns aircraft manufacturing companies, an oil company, airports, and even a uranium mining and production company. The provinces often own local airlines, electric power companies, telephone companies, mining companies, research laboratories, and construction firms.

Many of these government owned or controlled businesses show a profit. Others do not. Some may lose money year after year. But if it has been decided that an enterprise is essential to Canadian welfare, profitable or not, the people have been generally more prepared than Americans to have their government enter the economic marketplace as an owner and operator. To Canadians, the national airline is as much an essential service as the post office. If either or both make a profit, so much the better. If not, that does not make one less important than the other. The Canadian people and private Canadian business depend on both.

**Social services and medicare.** Canadians have generally approved their government's active role in Canadian business. They have also supported a larger network of public social services than exists in the United States. As in the United States, public education in Canada extends to the end of high school. But in Canada there are no longer any private universities. All universities depend on government support for the lion's share of their operating revenue. Although the universities set their own admission standards and charge tuition (usually much less than American universities), they are increasingly seen as part of the public education system.

Of all the areas in which Canadians have expanded their social service network, none is more important or costly than medicare. In 1961, the province of Saskatchewan was the first government in North America to introduce a medicare program for all its citizens. Before long, the federal government, in cooperation with all Canada's provinces, introduced a national program.

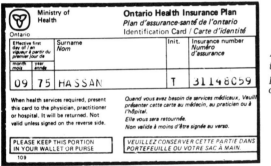

A card such as this is every Canadian's passport to medical care.

The specific operation of medicare varies from province to province. But every Canadian is entitled to the highest quality of medical care at public expense. This includes doctors, hospitals, and most medical support services such as ambulances, special medication, and home medical services. Medicare is seen as a right, not a privilege. No one goes without the best in medical care because of the cost. No one need rely on charity to pay medical bills. No family need fear that a member's unexpected or prolonged medical problems will cripple their financial security.

Doctors still must be paid. Hospital costs must be met. Every year they grow higher as new and often more expensive medical procedures are introduced. But Canadians feel these costs should not be borne by the sick individual or his family. Costs are covered by the community as a whole through government collection of a medical insurance premium from those who can afford it and through tax revenue. With the burden of medical costs lifted from their shoulders, it is hard for Canadians to remember a time when national medicare was not available to them.

It is true that medicare and the other social services Canadians have come to expect — a safety net protecting all Canadians — are very costly. Nevertheless, like a national railway or an electric power company, they are considered necessities, not luxuries. All Canadian citizens benefit. All share the cost. Whether costs will ever reach a point where services will have to be cut back for lack of funds remains to be seen. That will depend on the continuing strength of the Canadian economy.

**U.S. trade ties.** Nowhere is the influence of the United States on Canada felt more than in the field of economics. Today the two countries are one another's best trading partners. Canada sells almost three-quarters of all its exports to the United States. The United States does more business with Canada than it does with any other country. No two countries anywhere in the world are more closely linked economically.

For Canada, having a large nearby U.S. market for its exports is a great advantage. It can also pose some difficulties. It sometimes seems as if Canadian business is a hostage of the American buyer.

Recently, for example, there was a worldwide protest against Canadian seal hunters harvesting harp seal pups for their fur. To stop the seal hunt, environmental groups called on Americans to stop buying Canadian fish products in restaurants and supermarkets. Much of Canada's annual fish catch is exported to the United States. A successful American boycott could throw many thousands of Canadian fishermen, who have

*Greenpeace members spray young seals with harmless green dye to ruin the commercial value of the pelts.*

nothing to do with the seal hunt, out of work. Once again Canadians were reminded how vulnerable their economy is to American pressures.

There is yet another way in which the Canadian economy seems a hostage of its U.S. markets. Canada's economic strength depends largely on American prosperity. If the United States is prosperous, there is money available to buy Canadian raw material, food stuffs, and manufactured goods. If the American economy goes into a slump, purchases of Canadian exports are usually cut back. Canadian workers are laid off, Canadian businesses close, and the Canadian economy falters. Many Canadians would agree that, when the U.S. economy sneezes, the Canadian economy catches a cold.

But the economic flow is not all one way. Canada also imports food and manufactured goods from the United States.

**U.S. investment in Canada.** Because Canada is so close, so friendly, and so secure, many American companies have invested large sums of money there. They have expanded their business operations into Canada or bought Canadian companies. Today more than half of all Canadian business and industry is owned by American investors.

There is no doubt that American investment has been needed to develop the Canadian economy. Canada has a small population for its size, and Canadian investors do not have enough private financial resources for such a large task. U.S. investment remains important to Canadian growth. Canadians are fully aware of its benefits.

There has been a price to pay, however. Many Canadians are concerned that their country is becoming a branch plant of the U.S. economy. How, they wonder, will Canadians determine their own economic future if Americans control the economy?

*The Canadian flag flies over many branches of U.S. companies*

**The energy issue.** American control has recently been an especially vital issue in the Canadian oil and gas industry. Canada has large oil and gas fields in Alberta, Saskatchewan, and the Arctic. There are potential oil fields in the sea bed off the shores of Newfoundland and Nova Scotia.

But most oil companies in Canada are owned in whole or in large part by American companies. Are these companies, many Canadians wonder, apt to put Canadian interests first? Is oil too important a resource to allow non-Canadians to control it? How would Americans respond if oil and gas supplies within the United States were controlled by foreign companies? Would the American government or its people allow non-Americans to run this vital industry?

Another neighbor of the U.S., Mexico, has avoided this problem. In 1936, the government took over U.S.-owned oil companies in Mexico. The U.S. companies were paid for their losses, although not nearly as much as they claimed. A nationally owned company, Pemex, now controls oil and gas exploration, production, distribution, and export.

Canada recently set up its own nationally owned oil and gas company, Petro-Canada. It is still small compared with the major U.S. companies. It also does not have a monopoly. Petrocan coexists with the U.S. oil companies that dominate the industry.

For some time, the Canadian government has felt that more dramatic steps to Canadianize the vital energy industry were necessary. In 1980, it attempted to ensure Canadian control over oil and gas by introducing a National Energy Policy. All oil and gas companies operating in Canada had to be at least 51 percent Canadian owned.

American businesses protested. They argued that they had risked their money investing in Canada. Now

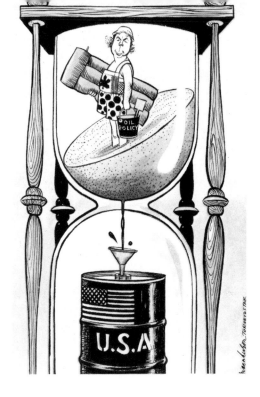

that there were profits to be made, they were being unfairly forced to sell out. They demanded that the U.S. government intervene. If Canada persisted with this policy, the companies wanted the United States to impose restrictions on Canadian imports, including gas and oil. If they went ahead with their National Energy Policy, Canadians might own the oil and gas but have no place to sell it. What is more, the U.S. firms threatened to close down all their Canadian exploration operations. This could have crippled the industry and stopped the vital search for new sources of gas and oil. The pressure was so great that the government retreated. The National Energy Policy was abandoned. Today, the Canadian oil and gas industry remains largely American owned.

The future of the economy, like the future of the country itself, remains unknown. But the signs are positive. Canadians share a sense of concern for Canada's future. With a wealth of natural resources and the dedication and caring of talented citizens, they can look forward with hope.

# Double-check

## Review

1. Which area of public social service in Canada is most important and most costly?

2. What fraction of its exports does Canada sell to the United States?

3. How much of Canadian business and industry is owned by American investors?

4. In which areas are Canada's large oil and gas fields located?

5. Name the Canadian government-owned oil and gas company.

## Discussion

1. In Canada a complex system of tax sharing between regions exists so that wealthier regions help support less fortunate regions. How do you suppose the wealthier regions feel about this system? How might the others feel? Do you think this system is a good one? Why or why not?

2. Every Canadian today is entitled to the highest quality medical care. How is the medical system different in the United States? What are the advantages and disadvantages of each?

3. Some Canadians have stated that the country is becoming a branch plant of the United States economy. Why? What does this mean to both Canadians and Americans?

## Activities

1. Canada has made many contributions in medicine, science, and technology. Students might be interested in finding out more about Canadian achievements and the Canadians who have been involved.

2. The pros and cons of foreign investments in Canada might be listed from the Canadian point of view. Students might compare their lists and discuss how they would feel if they were Canadian.

3. The class might organize a debate on whether the Canadian government should control all oil and natural gas resources.

# Skills

## CANADIANS AT WORK

| Type of Industry | % of Labor Force |
|---|---|
| **Natural Resources** | |
| Farming | 5.2 |
| Fishing/trapping | 0.2 |
| Lumbering | 0.8 |
| Mining | 1.4 |
| **Production** | |
| Manufacturing | 21.0 |
| Building | 6.5 |
| **Services** | |
| Business | 17.5 |
| Finance | 4.9 |
| Government services | 6.9 |
| Transportation/communication/utilities | 8.7 |
| Other (legal, medical, personal) | 26.9 |
| **TOTAL** | **100.0** |

Source: Statistics Canada

*Use the chart above and information in Chapter 16 to answer the following questions.*

1. What do the figures in the above chart represent?

2. Which natural resource industry employs the most people?
   (a) mining  (b) forestry  (c) agriculture

3. What percentage of Canada's labor force works in production industries?
   (a) 27.5%  (b) 17.5%  (c) 6.5%

4. Suppose a person works on an assembly line, helping to make cars. Under which main heading would this person's work belong?
   (a) Natural Resources  (b) Production  (c) Services

5. Which of the following people work in service industries?
   (a) farmers and fishermen  (b) radio announcers and doctors
   (c) carpenters and bricklayers

PHOTO AND ART CREDITS: • Cover, 186, Brian Willer/MacLeans • 8, 54, Government of British Columbia • 11, Stelco Inc. • 12, 110, 196, 205, 213, 223, The Toronto Star • 18, 37, 38, 86, Direction generale du Tourisme, Quebec • 20, 32, 33, Tourism New Brunswick, Canada • 24, 42, 43, 161, 190, NFB Phototeque ONF • 27, 28, Government of Newfoundland and Labrador • 30, Rick Buncombe • 42, CN Tower/The Niagara Parks Commission • 49, 50, 65, 182 Travel Manitoba • 51, 52, Travel Alberta/Edmonton Klondike Days Association • 56, B.C. Place • Becky Striegler, Whitehorse Star • 141, Photo Features Ltd./NDP • 147, Ontario Hydro • 156, 157, Stan Stevens, Ottawa/Andres-Newton, Ottawa • 159, Art Gallery of Ontario, Gift of the Klamer Family Collection, 1978 • 171, 177, 182, Multicultural History Society of Ontario • 197, Canapress Photo Service • 206, CFRB • 210, Merle Tingley, The London Free Press • 215, Spar Aerospace Limited • 220, Pierre Gleizes/Greenpeace • 221, Ford Motor Company. The following are courtesy of Public Archives Canada: 41, C-11369; 62, C-122384; 64, C-25702; 67, C-5136, C-17727, C-11226, C-69709; 69, C-70256; 71, C-2401; 72, C-70263; 73, C-73431; 75, C-13585; 80, C-5746; 81, C-17338; 84, C-19584; 91, C-20756; 97, C-70244; 99, C-1993, C-5414; 101, C-5438, C-5456; 103, C-73666; 106, C-7299; 107, C-21873; 113, C-21290; 114, C-1070; 116, C-6727; 119, PA-120150; 120, C-1879; 125, PA-113850; 130, PA-1654, PA-1027; 132, C-18864; 135, C-29396, C-34024; 141, C-66639; 142, PA-132468; 144, PA-132727; 148, PA-122737; 152, PA-122562; 164, C-45121; 170, PA-10255, C-19935; 171, C-22217; 175, PA-27943; 176, PA-34015; 179, PA-124866; 182, C-45088; 188, C-30085; 189, C-104125; 194, C-33320; 196, C-112876; 223, C-112970.

# Notes

# Notes

# Notes

# Notes

# Notes

# Notes